IN A *World*
OF THEIR
OWN

EIGHT MATRIXES OF SUPERSTAR
PERFORMERS OF PERPETUITY

FREDERICK K.
LANCASTER B.A, J.D.

outskirtspress

DENVER, COLORADO

In a World of Their Own
Eight Matrixes of Superstar Performers of Perpetuity
All Rights Reserved.
Copyright © 2014 Frederick K. Lancaster B.A, J.D.
v2.0

Outskirts Press, Inc.
http://www.outskirtspress.com

ISBN: 978-1-4327-9925-0

Outskirts Press and the "OP" logo are trademarks belonging to Outskirts Press, Inc.

PRINTED IN THE UNITED STATES OF AMERICA

"…I want it said of me
by those who knew me best,
that I always plucked a thistle
and planted a flower
where I thought a flower would grow."

~Abraham Lincoln

To Nicole, may this year, 2014, bring you the fullness of joy and happiness.

Frederick K. Lancaster

Acknowledgments

I would like to acknowledge these individuals: my parents, Emma Q. Lancaster and the late Dr. Herman J. Lancaster, who were my first superstar performers. To my girls: sisters Jacquelyn, Hermanstine, and Ocela; and to my nieces, Christian, Imani, and Za'cario, as well as to my lady, Rhonda Myers. To my brother-in-law, Willie Dension. To my spiritual little brothers, Shawn "Stringbean" William, Tyrone Dunn, and Tony Glover; my spiritual big brother Mike Davis, and his wife Delia. Thanks for making your home a home away from home. To my friend Vince Lauria and his wife Darleene. I acknowledge as well my spiritual little sister Michelle Hudson, and my spiritual big sister Joyce Canty; thank you all for your encouragement.

For my parents:
Emma Q. Lancaster and the late Dr. H.J. Lancaster

Table of Contents

Section I

The Prologue

I am nine years old. It is a Saturday morning, and I am sitting in front of the television at my house. In fact, many other young boys my age have become the high priests of TV-watching on these Saturday mornings. Some watch the familiar cartoons; some fancy other shows. I prefer watching the old black and white movies. For reasons unknown, these kinds of movies fascinate me. Drawn to them as if moved by command on an Ouija board, my brain waves easily accept what I am seeing. At first, their appeal is visual—wrapped in the celluloid context of movie-making—but I eventually come away believing that there is much more here, and more than a fantasy world. I experience, above all, a gripping and mesmerizing feeling when I see the actors on that screen. Arguably, I believe and feel at a much deeper subconscious level, nudging me beyond the sights and sounds.

So then, after taking inventory of these feelings, I come to realize that the attraction is some of both—a nudge from a deeper level, and the sparkle of the sights and sounds. Sure, I am impressed by the sights and sounds of what I am watching, but I also see something beyond that. I see authenticity, a rather soulful existence that can come only from people who know themselves well enough, how their talents work, and who have control of their own personal power.

This revelation thrusts me into a different place in my thinking. Then all of a sudden I experience the thought of that elusive "IT" quality. At an early age, it dawns on me, for the first time, that the energy I experience is, in essence, that "IT" quality—the one, you know, that makes you say:

I cannot put my hands on "IT," but there is something that makes this moment or this person special beyond their obvious talents. And that childhood experience sparks my interest in exploring this "IT" quality.

One might call that "IT" spiritual, or identify it as a person's highest potential, or simply embrace it as the hand of God at work. On the other hand, one might acknowledge this "IT" in terms of a person understanding of their will and mission, carried out in their natural and highest fashion.

In any event, now that I am an adult, I have received a glimpse of that exclusive "IT" many times. I witnessed it in great actors who when watching them glide across the screen with ease and eloquence in one of their movies. I could witness it in another actor whose commanding panther-like stride, or the extreme confidence in a daring actress exuded. Of course, I have seen "IT" in politicians, businesspersons, athletes, teachers, and even scientists. At first, "IT" is an eye-catching moment—a flicker, a spark—but close examination dictates that something of a higher order of skill training is at work. I also gathered that, by and large, this exclusive "IT" is available to all, but there is a price to pay.

Further examination, however, eventually led me to look closer at the lives of these individuals I admired, to see what really made their lives special. This turning point soon allowed me to grow out of the stargazing and the fanciful spin to which I had become accustomed, and I began to view these people's lives with deeper sincere meaning. It is important to note that screen actors were not my only frame of reference. However, they are useful for conducting various explanations in this book—explanations that show how a common pattern exists amongst many other superstars in various fields. However, in the end, individuals in the fields of visual aesthetic and performance, who were admired and lauded, gave me every reason to choose them as the perfect subject matter for discussion and examination. And although I have used a number of vocations to make my point in this book, for the most part, celebrity is one subject that appeals across practically all professions. If truth be told, a number of professions—ranging from politics to business, sports, and even education—have adopted marketing tools similar to the entertainment industry. We cannot deny this fact.

Being a celebrity, as we know, has a tendency to attract our attention more than anything else. So it became easy for me to use celebrities as a point of reference. However, my examination became less focused on their celebrity and talent, and more on the personal qualities that allowed them to use their talents in such a way as to expand and highlight their humanity. I then began to draw from a set of principles that I saw to be similar in other well-known people whom I saw as ordinary people doing extraordinary things. I thought this was enough for me to further my investigation.

I examined several areas influencing these individuals. I wanted to know what motivated them, who influenced their lives the most, what personal standards they operated by, and why others wanted to pattern their lives after them. My answers came through researching several dozen high-level performers whom I was familiar with, and seizing upon their shared common set of systems (matrixes, I called them) that distinguish them from others. I then had insight into why certain people are deemed superstar performers when others—who may look and act the role of a superstar performer—are not.

The answers did not come, as one might think, based on the fame, prestige, or money these people might have had; nor did obtaining material riches give them any greater status or lift into this special class. What I discovered, instead, were certain ingrained qualities acquired only through an environment that was deemed loving, challenging, accepting, and appreciative of their talent and their acts of humanity. Similar to the wearing or holding of a good luck charm, or a rosary in their hands for a keepsake, I discovered they guarded and honored particular values within themselves that were as cherished by them in the same way that some may value a car, a boat, or a house.

Yet the prevalent thinking has been that superstar performers live for their craft—and it is logical to assume that this is the case, but truth be told, it's more important for them to *preserve themselves and those qualities that make them special.* Their talent, in other words, becomes an alter ego for expressing their humanity. Soon it dawned on me that their talent functioned more as a vehicle to express their worldview, and above all, it represented their highest self-expression.

In the pages that follow, I intend to share with you what I have come to discover about what makes a legendary superstar. I will admit from the outset that being influential has some impact on superstardom, but being influential does not necessarily mean recognition, riches, or prestige, as we have come to believe. If this were the case, then we could pluck many well-known people from tabloid news magazines who are influential just due to being rich and famous.

On the other hand, perfection is not the carrying card of the superstar performer either. They come with flaws—bad habits and personal shortcomings. However, this work does not evaluate those flaws. It does examine authentic greatness that, at times, is at odds with the present definition of greatness. This definition often is hidden in obscure layers, but has the simple message and lesson taught by a high school math teacher, who may have influenced a number of the geniuses who are captains of technology today; or a drama teacher who may have inspired a well known actor, or an Academy Award winning actress. It is possible that none of these mentors would ever receive the honor of greatness that their pupils received, but they still would be great—they would be superstars.

Yet the question arose: Would any of these teachers, or even a firefighter, be considered superstars too? This was one-half of the debate. The other half was determining how they shared the same ecosystem of values, conditions, and innate qualities that legendary superstar performers share. In other words, what consistently made superstars dwell *In a World of Their Own?* What helped them maintain their robust careers and influence for decades, even when they were not churning out the performances they had once enjoyed?

For instance, I would be comfortable in saying that any one of the prolific songwriters of the sixties, have influenced a plethora of songwriters and musicians for several generations, even though much of their most prolific work dates back to the 1960s. Their continuing work today—though not as prolific before—is as significant, and continues to influence many top songwriters. Being signed to a particular record label, may well receive credit for many other artists' desire to be signed to that label their idol made as his home.

In any event, by researching volumes of information, I drew some conclusions about what really determines a superstar performer, and the qualities that make them this way. I came away also understanding what qualities people should be looking for when forming organizations. In my opinion, the information I have shared in these pages can be useful to any number of professional mentors, including a talent agent, a sports agent, or any other personal management position. I believe the information that I am sharing with you is information that has helped me, as I wrote this book. Writing this book was as therapeutic for me as anything I have ever done. I prefer to think of this book in terms of a workbook rather than as an instructional manual. I would not advocate something to others unless I believed in it myself or came upon it through my own experience and observations. Secondly, the concepts are easy to understand, but they are also difficult to apply consistently.

I learned as well that far too many people who have innate talents fall short of their superstardom because they bend too easily to vices that disrupt their progress and get them off their game. I believe a person who disciplines themselves with simple and consistent routines will eventually reach effective performance. Thirdly, the matrixes outlined should be practically applied; they are not presented as a quick fix. You will come away knowing as you read them that they are familiar. Think of them as guideposts on your journey. Although the concepts are likely to be familiar, what may be different are the angles from which I present them, and the ways in which they are explained.

Fourth, the matrixes are solid qualities that have endured. One may call them virtues, values, principles, or whatever you feel is comfortable for you.

My sense is that by understanding the matrixes that are common amongst true superstar performers, you will appreciate what it takes to become one and therefore begin the journey to acquire these characteristics.

After considering a number of qualities that might have made the eight-matrix list, I found the following consistent amongst many of the superstar performers. They are: *Standards, Integrity, Honesty, Passion, Preparation, Talent, Support System,* and *Community.* Clearly, one can see that these are concepts familiar to management, leadership, and personal improvement.

Nevertheless, do not be deceived into thinking that they are simple terms. When applied to the lives of those considered superstar performers , the concepts are used multi-dimensionally. What if I say, for instance, that Johnny grew up in Little Italy, New Jersey and grew up with the customs and culture of an Italian-American family. The Italian-American neighborhood adopted certain codes of honor that were expected from your neighborhood, your culture, and your family. If you lied or snitched, you would be punished—not only severely by the kids in the neighborhood, but perhaps also by your parents. Moreover, if you had brothers, you might have received a beat-down from them. Whoever lived in that set ecosystem knew what to expect and knew the consequences if they crossed those lines, but because they were aware of the consequences, they would be less inclined to do it again. They learned the standards of the ecosystem, through conditioning. What happened here is that there had always existed a core standard, but the community expanded it to reflect their shared expectations.

This did not redefine the concept of standards, but it did expand its dimensions. It did not allow one to narrow the definition to fit a generic concept of standards. Far too often, when people look at a concept, they are looking at it in the form in which they perceive it, or looking at it as what they believe it means. For example, the word "principle" is a concept and virtue that is accorded the highest esteem in its meaning. It means different things in different contexts. Principle for the priest is different than principle for the thief. While the priest might hold a certain principle, the thief holds a certain principle too. While the priest may be kind in walking an old lady across the street, making sure she is safe, the thief will do the same, except that at the end of his walking her, he will knock her over the head and take her purse. As perplexing as words may be, the language we use may not mean what we think it means. However, we can all agree, most of the time, that when we speak in certain terms we come into proximity of its real meaning.

Therefore, take stock when looking at the matrixes; consider looking at the totality of the circumstances. I am not simply changing the language or meaning, but expanding it, as you will find in reading about in this book. The expanding language does not adopt new concepts; it allows people to look inside the world of the person whom you are viewing, and allows you to see it from their point of view or from different angles. It's like the "looking glass principle," in which the person viewing his situation in a three-way prism, looks to the viewer who's viewing him, and see what he sees, but is able to view it the way it is in his own reality. By and large, it will become clearer as you read further that there are different methods by which superstar performers process their vision, but they are still able to meet at the same apex in achieving it.

You will hear the term "superstar performer" repeated many times, like a mantra. In addition to this, you will become familiar with other terms related to the superstar performer—terms as *support system, intimate circle, go-fer, independent contractor*, and *the associates' circle* are all terms that one will become acquainted with when going through this journey.

Again, my basic intent in this book aims toward providing strategies for those who manage people, in order to engage in serious evaluation and conversation with them. The manifest function of the evaluation determines, when evaluating a relationship—whether business or otherwise—does it align directly with one's core values? If you break it all down, this book is simply about relationships. I am urging people to question the motives of the individuals they form relationships with, both professionally and personally, and begin to set ground rules for those expectations.

It definitely gives one pause that if one becomes fortunate enough to collaborate with a person who has enormous talent, but later finds that they are sordid and void of conscience, this should be a red flag for you to ditch that collaboration. In fact, you should run as fast as you can, because nothing in the world is going to fix or change this situation.

Therefore, a word of caution should apply here, in that business relationships are to be treated as marriages, except there is no kissing (you can see me laughing). They should be guarded with the same care as any other relationship, because they have similar dynamics as those discussed in this book. One will not be surprised to find that successful superstar performers become successful because they have held long, enduring partnerships with people with similar values and visions.

The last section of this book, entitled *How to Build a Superstar Performer from the Ground Up,* is not a blueprint for succeeding as a superstar performer, but it offers a specific understanding of the habits and or routines customary to those performers who succeed. *Conditioning,* therefore, should be the word that jumps out at you when clarifying what is at the root of their professional success, and their personal success. The greatest understanding, perhaps, that I hope you take from this book is that superstardom is far from the follies that we currently give credence to when observing the ridiculous actions of people who brand themselves as true talent, but don't do the work. It is much more, and I hope you come to an understanding of the difference.

"Hey, Over Here"

(The birth of stargazing and its destructive effect on productivity in the arts.)

By today's standards, the well-oiled publicity machine, once the proud rumor mill of the Golden age of Hollywood, has become a sophisticated high-tech world of convergent media, where the internet bloggers, Twitter, and many web users rule the world of cyberspace. The inventions created by these extraordinary tools have allowed content holders to transmit dialogue faster than you can blink. These wonderful apparatus have provided enormous power to a legion of reporters, bloggers, and freelancers in ways that have made average techies into famous household names.

The reporting provided by these individuals—true or not—has enabled them to game the Hollywood system into small armies comprised of informants, would-be friends, ex-friends, nannies, bodyguards, and causal friends to do one important thing—to simply "snitch." In fact, the role of the system today is less insular than it was in the infancy of movie-making. Due in part to the current technology available, makes it possible for the exes, who are eager to reveal X-rated tapes of their mates, to do this shamelessly in order to make money. During earlier Hollywood days, the studio and the actor's handlers were able to quash this kind of retribution from a mate. They were able to silence the noise of potential fallout by appealing to that person's spouse, with an eye toward protecting the actor's brand. Then again, some of these celebrities themselves participate in this type of sport, which even by today standards, is considered tame and part of the job. Furthermore, the growing celebrity news gossip outlets, from Access Hollywood, to Showbiz Tonight and TMZ, have all used their inside connections to seek access, creating an industry within an industry.

Nevertheless, before there existed others who have made fame and fortune off celebrity excesses, there were the original snitches called gossip colunmist . These well-connected people who utilized their inside resources in order to create a system where celebrity fame became a business. Many of these colunmist knew the film stars personally because they perhaps had experience in the theater. Their well connections enabled them to become skilled at creating a pipeline of information to their doorsteps. In an era where the studio system controlled and guarded its stars' images, these colunmist received rare and unique access into the private lives and scoops on the biggest stars at that time. During a period when most major stars were under exclusive contracts—sometimes as long as seven years—and bound by strict morality clauses, these special brand of colunmist were able to uncover mountains of salacious information on them. The information they uncovered, however, came at the expense of their careers and livelihood, where investigations revealed information damaging to their personas.

Many of these colunmist haunted a well beloved actor obsessively pertaining to his political views and weakness for younger women. It is said that their relentless pursuits contributed to his leaving the USA. Though this type of activity drove many in the industry to shame, today these identical escapades are regular fodder for consumer demand.

Many articles they wrote provided insight into the trysts of the stars of that day. Despite the studio's insistence on guarding their contract players' image, there still lurked the snitches and the handlers of that day, who had little control over what got out, and who bowed to the mercy of these snitches. In contrast to what happens today, if a performer was rumored to be a homosexual or having multiple affairs, it remained a secret within the studio system. If a performer was an admitted heroin addict, the code between those in the industry was to keep it silent. If it was revealed that someone had leaked out information considered unauthorized to give, that person was immediately blacklisted. The small community of Hollywood had its rules, but with such powerful foes as the ones who had exclusive inside information, those rules did not apply in giving them exclusivity.

Even in an era that is less-inhibited, the fame game sometimes overrides common sense and decency, where anything goes. Nowadays, everyone is trying to get in the fame game; it's not the exclusive territory of the snitches, who have now been joined by the less-talented D-listers who come to the arena and have joined in.

One famous star has been reported as saying, "There's never any bad publicity." In her view, if you can be seen, no matter how bad the light may be, it is still considered good publicity. The truth of this fact is clearly seen today, in reality shows, which thrive on cat fights and drama, and in "anything goes" shock effect episodes on television. Then again, many have seen this behavior play-out before. During the 1920ths through the 1930th's, a generation of women known as *Flappers*, exhibited a similar don't care attitude in most everything they did. Their well-documented excesses still amaze people today and would fit well with modern day over the top stunts. *Flappers* were known to have ravenous appetites for sex, smoking, carousing, and out of bounds risky behavior. If a well-established man wanted a willing mistress to have an affair with, these women were the ones to ask. Before women ever though of not wearing underwear, they were the first to do so (which by today's standards is common). Flashing became a common activity. Cocaine and heroin use was a common occurrence, as well as, entertaining the notion of having sex with anyone they found attractive or who asked.

In an era where exhibitionist behaviors were prohibited, these women broke the norms with reckless disregard for the consequences of their actions, without any shame. Although nobody could deny that they made their own rules, their behavior lent itself to insights about troubling problems that haunted them.

The period between the 1920s and 1930s was marked with excessive follies. Between bootlegging and Prohibition, a mindset came around of "anything goes"—and similar excesses would be seen thirty years later. Yet in spite of the permissiveness of the age, a bad reputation still counted as a liability, and in the system of Hollywood business where an actor relied heavily on their audience, if they failed to capture them because of an actor's private life, it meant serious damage to the industry and the studio to which they were contracted. This became important, since the period marked a weeding-out of winners, losers, and those who were casualties at the hand of their own whims. For what was about to occur signified a "change a-coming." Furthermore, right at the start of the 1930s a new moral code was ushered in to Hollywood, patterned after the famous production codes established by Willie Hayes.

Production codes, however, were rules to govern guidelines in censorship on the movie sets in a vast majority of major motion picture releases between 1930 and 1968. The production codes never censored conduct of the performers' personal lives, but it was implied to them in many other ways that they must exercise caution. As discussed earlier, studios implemented a moral clause in their actors' contracts to lessen embarrassment for them. These efforts were meant to insulate their behavior. Contrary to those efforts and the tight rein studios had on the reputations of its stars, their follies still continued, and when their guards were down, an army of reporters came center stage to write about them.

Some major movie stars remained protective of their careers, and had more to lose by being a contract player than lesser-known actors and actresses. The situation is different today; there are fewer threats from a studio-style system, and the army of tell-alls does not lack subject matter or have any scruples in reporting on the peccadilloes of the famous. In addition, there is no shortage of snitches willing to sell information. Yet another interesting novelty to report on is that some performers today now have skin in the game in the baiting for bids from columnists and photographers to take the first pictures, and get the first scoops of their private affairs for a payday.

Let us take for instance the current bidding between some celebrities and their handlers to see who is willing to pay the highest price for the first photos or stories about a new child. We are used to accepting the peddling of this commodity as part of the auctioning process, since it has become an arm of the entertainment machinery, but what's most alarming in this context is the current generation's mistaken acceptance of such actions as an reasonable goal to reach. It reinforces the theory in which tripe is rewarded more than good work. Another thing it does, as well, is invite the notion that any publicity is good publicity, even if it results in embarrassment. In my opinion, it is one thing to participate in this kind of activity once in a while; it is another thing to make a living at it. It suggests to some that it is okay to act in this manner as long as fame is the prize that awaits them. For this reason, privacy and modesty are not valued.

One fascinating point to note regarding the celebrity phenomenon is that it is never in dispute when it comes to young people chasing of the brass ring. They will do almost anything for it. What is discovered is that young people's desire for fame overrides the serious work necessary to accomplish value-driven goals. Even though it is fine to be award fame for good work, what is not fine is if generations of young people claim entitlement to fame without work. Does this affirm the current outcry made by young people who are spoiled, and clamor for anything within their reach? On the other hand, are they in a state of vertigo, spinning in distorted views of reality? These questions need to be answered.

Therefore, part of what we will be discussing and evaluating in this work indirectly relates to their claims. In addition, though being an instant celebrity possibly rewards one with some temporary relief, does this immediacy stand the test of time? Will such people become another shooting star lost among other shooting stars whose talents might have gained traction and benefited the world more broadly if they had used them in a productive fashion? The scope of this work is in essence meant to examine those differences, and frame theories on what makes some performers' names synonymous with solid workmanship that puts them in *A World of Their Own*.

While others chose to wallow in the mire of celebrity, I examined the qualities and the matrixes that matter for those who manage people.

I understand the reasoning in exploiting individuals for financial gain as the norm, and there is a multitude of avenues to accomplish this act. It is also true that an environment that continues to feed an audience with less than quality work cheapens that art. This work celebrates serious work by serious people, appealing to the ones who work with talent, to resist working with individuals whose motives and intent to have quick paydays and take shortcuts to stardom lead to nowhere. In the end, this reminds us that good work does pay off after all, and we will do best in refraining from giving license to those who proudly stand on the corner and announce, "Hey , over here."

Skill Trainers v. Non-Skill Trainers

Audiences find it fascinating when they can peer into the private lives of their favorite celebrities and witness the breakdown of their relationships. A stumble or an embarrassing misstep is something that both the viewing audience and the media love. For the media, it becomes a game that they are more than willing to play, and for those in print, it serves to incite a rise from its readers as a means to selling more papers. For many others who view these train wrecks from the sidelines, it is like watching a drama at the theater. Yet the ones who are the objects of the attention still occasionally play along with the game, providing enough theatrics in order for them to receive cash for it. Although these events render immediate gratification in the short term, they are like any addiction and vice that trolls on people's desperation and insecurities. Today, as it might have been in the past, it appears that these are normal functions of the entertainment industry, which has accepted trade-baiting as part of the landscape. The difference today, however, is that participants use and abuse what has been given to them in order to exploit its wealth, without making any worthy contribution to the system.

Evidence of this use and abuse is prevalent by current standards in many reality shows, in which persons are willing to embarrass themselves at length for the sake of the brass ring. The major reward, by most accounts, for being on a reality show is generally to show how ruthless, exploitative, authoritative, selfish, self-serving, and vain you can be. It becomes less about how skillful one may be, and more about how much one is paid to pretend to act without acting. The requirement and/or criterion become not talent, but self-loathing. For the most part, these individuals aren't skill trainers, but lesser skill trainers—wanna-bes. Moreover, the value systems that they espouse tend to do damage to the ones who are serious about their craft and desire to contribute meaning to their community. This becomes exactly the reason why managers or agents should take significant stock of their motives when they work with talent, and step back and be determined to evaluate what is best for their client's future.

I seriously doubt that any of our rock and roll royalty would place their brand on anything without their managers consent or methodically questioning the reasoning behind the motives and how it would affect their career or brand in the long term. It is in the same vein that one U.S. President conducts a Socratic exercise with another President in questioning how he would approach a major crisis. Often, managers never think this way in their deliberations, especially in times when there is economic strain and when it is tempting to exploit clients for quick gain. One miscalculation of some shady deal can manifest itself immediately and negatively affect the entire future of the company. Regardless of the route one takes with their career, they must first and always consider the longevity of it.

For a person who is a serious player in his profession, it comes down to making critical decisions about whether one should dedicate time and energy to certain performances for cash while attempting to keep one's self-respect.

We all can probably agree that skill trainers are at the top of the food chain. They are describe in the book *Talent Is Overrated,* persons who in a deliberate manner make concerted efforts in practicing their craft. In other words, they have great intensity in focusing on the prize. In addition, they also have identified what they do well, have chosen a craft suitable to their talents, and are willing to work at it to perfection. The action that skill trainers take to exercise their craft is never easy; nor is it without resistance. In Howard Gardner's book *Creating Minds he conducted* a case study of Sigmund Freud, pointing out Freud's amazing intellect, but also his insatiable thirst for knowledge. Freud read widely and mastered many subjects, but prepared himself well. In other words, learning a cross-section of subject matter gave breadth and depth to his mind, allowing him to stretch himself in ways he would not otherwise have done.

A few NBA players are known for their many rituals of practicing shooting after their games and are diligent and prodigious workers off-season. Stories are told of many of them sitting on the top bleachers, shooting balls to the basketball goal. Many, I am sure, didn't always enjoy the repetitive cadence of doing the same drills over and over, but they knew it was necessary to stay efficient at their skill. The simple action taken by these skill trainers in preparing themselves, while considered a physical extrinsic task, is performed with intrinsic intent in mind. By applying due diligence to their work, the process reveals its secrets to them because they have done the necessary work to reveal them. Furthermore, passion becomes another element that drives them, not fame; however, if fame occurs because of their efforts, it becomes a partial reward for their good deed. It simply does not dictate their cause, purpose, or vision. The intensity of their work carries with it an immense ebb and flow, twenty-four hours a day.

Many of these NBA superstars lives extend far beyond their shooting a ball on the court. Though evidence showed that some lived for the game of basketball, other things defined them. They measured their superstardom by improving the lives of others and helping young people understand the intangibles that the game of basketball taught them. Whether these superstar performers were in the realm of top business people, actors, directors, musicians, or writers, these types of people are a true manager's dream.

But keep this in mind that a performer's motivation is intrinsic—meaning that it goes well beyond the surface of fame and fortune. This notion is well in line with much of the research done on lasting achievers. Teresa Annabel in her research has examined this important point—whether extrinsically motivated individuals are bad news for those who aspire to high and significant achievement. We sometimes see this amongst reality show contestants. Individuals who follow this frame of mind and *fame of mind* are motivated sometimes by only selfish reasons, and due to their actions and motives, their contributions may ring hollow. The intrinsic elements that I am prescribing here are true virtues of craftsmanship among most skill trainers, even if their routines to become better skill trainers appear extrinsic in nature.

The acquisition of money is often the source of extrinsic motivation. The desperate attempt to acquire it has many levels. One motivation, obviously, is to pay bills, but also might be to help an ill relative, friend, or any other deserving cause. Other times, the quest becomes extrinsic, but intrinsic by purpose.

For example, a famous coach who once taught me sociology in college told his college class, pertaining to the topic of moral justification, that he didn't see anything wrong in a young woman taking her clothes off to strip. If it meant paying for her tuition for college, then she was no different from a person working at McDonald's to accomplish the same.

His justification, thinking, and psychology are predicated on the notion of no barriers existing except the ones those persons place on themselves. Whether those barriers were moral, physical, or spiritual, for the most part, those persons determined their own limits and were able to work through them, instead of depending on someone else. At the end, the result was the same: graduation from college, with the prospect of getting a good job. The result alleviated the need for the student to strip or to flip burgers; extrinsic conduct mirrored intrinsic need.

Therefore, it is crucial to understand that from a "bird's-eye view," when an activity appears extrinsic, the desires, motives, and passion may be intrinsic by purpose. Understanding this point becomes one of the important factors that drive many superstar performers.

If a manager or agent wants to identify whether he has a true skill trainer in his midst, try finding out who that person's mentors are, and what their qualities are. Generally, one replicates the habits, rituals, and work ethics of great individuals.

Unlike some reality show wanna-bes (you notice I said some) the sum game is like a person wandering in the wilderness without a true compass. However, I have to admit—and this is hard to confess—there are reality shows that exemplify quality programming *and* teach us values.

If a reality show appears truthful in its documentation, portraying a person's or family's life in a struggle, but details solutions toward victory, I can see value in its content. In this case, human conflict is always an interesting experiment to dissect, and it has its usefulness in showing people how to overcome challenges in their lives and succeeding when odds are against them. These types of examples are character-builders, but mere mayhem without direction or substance is never worthwhile.

In order to avoid sounding naïf, I will say that I realize shows of this kind reap enormous revenue for the networks, and are cheap to make. On the other hand, they also send a strong message to the many ill-equipped individuals who audition for shows such as these, to act in ways that do not support their best interest. Those shows are the exact platforms that attract the onslaught of the wanna-bes…non-skill trainers, who desire something for nothing. With an avaricious desire to be "eye candy," they will attempt increasingly outrageous and stupid acts to be noticed.

I ask potential managers and agents to consider this question: Is this the type of person you want to represent? I ask another question as well: Would a respectable agency worth their salt invest their time and money in a person who makes a fool of himself in this manner? If the answer is yes, good luck! For some, this might be an ingenious way of attracting management to see your raw talent once you unpeel the facades. My guess would be that a self-respecting manager would do well to stay away from these types of individuals if they are serious about their clients and themselves. In my opinion, there are easier ways to determine whether you have a legitimate client. (Many examples will be described in the eight matrixes in this text.) One way of determining whether that is the case is if there exists an intimate connection between highly creative people, and intrinsically motivated ones: a trait rarely defined with non-skill trainers. Secondly, the skill trainer's risk factor is significantly different from the non-skill trainer's. For example, some will suggest that for an individual to subject him or herself to public humiliation in front of a national audience takes an enormous amount of courage and risk. It is true that there is some risk here when the raw self can be revealed and one can make fun of one's imperfections to an audience in an embarrassing way. One might even lose his or her self-respect in the process for being less than a serious-minded person, but perceived as a clown. The action of the person may even have been an exercise of empowerment. These are a number of theories to ponder. But I tend to err on the side that those humiliating acts people perform on television—as hilarious as they appear—don't count for much; nor are they losing anything, since many may not have much self-respect to lose.

What one should ask these people, however, is why they do what you do, and how important the gains and losses are to that person? If you fall on your face for falling on your face, you have not lost anything.

The hurt of a minor rejection on a dating show is a genuine loss, if the aim is to find a true love or one's soul mate. However, the losses endured by skill trainers appear different. It is, instead, an intense exercise of love of their art. A skill trainer has dedicated long hours of work to his or her craft, along with the risk of no guarantee of success. It is both a lonely pursuit and a blissful exodus, knowing that the time put into the craft, and the focus thereof, will deliver what he expects. Moreover, time spent by skill trainers has a higher order of risk attached to it than that of the wannabe-non-skill trainers. In the skill trainers' world, there is a constant deliberate practice of their craft and nurturing of it that comes with a heavy price. They are too busy focusing on other matters to be consumed with chasing the brass ring, which, to them, may or may not result in recognition, but there is no mistake in the clarity of their purpose.

On the other hand, the non-skill-trainers damage too much of themselves to be taken seriously when indulging in activities that are not in line with their "true north." In fact, there might come a time when a non-skill-trainer will want to reveal his or her true talent. But this may have come at the worst moment to be taken seriously because of their prior actions. At all times, effective performers guard themselves from frivolous activity.

In a memorable scene from *On the Waterfront,* Terry Mallory, played by Marlon Brando, has a conversation with his brother Charley, played by Rod Steiger while riding in a cab. A special intensity occurs between the two brothers that highlights that blood is not thicker than water. Those who have viewed the movie can only see the relationship between the two brothers as similar to a toxic relationship between a manager and his client.

There is a sense of irony and wisdom in that for those who have their client's best interest at heart. They should, instead, be mandated to take on the Hippocratic oath as doctors do, to "Do no harm," in sending their client into a lion's den of activities that neither complements nor enhances his or her talents. It is similar to killing the goose that laid the golden egg. Even worse, it can be like sending them into a den of thieves. One notable coach, whose record obtained as head coach of a major university that still stands today, was a great mentor of men. The influence he had on the development of his players pertains to the spirit of this text.

He advised those who aspired to be mentors that they must first gain respect, but more than anything, they should not change the person whom they are mentoring, but help them to become a better person.

Throughout this text, keep this thought in mind. Keying in on this sentiment will clear the brush off the path toward understanding what one should aim toward, and in the next chapters give to you the eight qualities that identify people of effective performance. In reading and analyzing these matrixes, it will dawn on you that you have known many individuals with the same qualities in your own life, and hopefully one day you will come to develop them in yourself.

Section II
The Eight Matrixes

Matrix #1: Unique Standards

I initially thought I actually understood the concept of standards before I researched it. Before then, perhaps like many others, I considered it similar to a moral compass. This view was entirely misguided. What I discovered is that standards can be identified as a combination of virtues drawn from a number of concepts. Though I partially accepted the broader views of standards to include ethical standards, moral standards, business standards, standards of operations, and even standard virtues, I still came away not understanding much, until I began to find that one common fact they all shared was the element of *conduct*. Not right conduct, or moral conduct, but simply conduct—a kind of conduct whose standard helps one reach a level of excellence. This is not just any conduct, but high conduct, and one where the standards are governed by one's own rules, rather than others'.

This kind of conduct is noteworthy for superstar performers.

Standards don't always mean the same thing for everyone. Yet by and large, we often make statements in terms of standards, as if we know what they mean. In fact, because those terms are repeated so often, we have come to think of them as self-evident.

For the purpose of this text, standards will be thought of on personal bases. Instead of seeing standards in the broader sense, I am more inclined to see it in an authoritative and narrower view, not over others, but of oneself. I believe this definition gives us a window into the personal ownership of superstars. It fits well within the core definition of a standard that most of us understand and can agree upon. It also literally means walking in one's own faith and vision, while defying conventional thought. Yet in no way does this indicate that one should act in ways that are fancy-free or irresponsible regarding their gifts. It does mean—when it comes to superstar performing—acting responsible with the gift you were given in its highest form.

In my opinion, the concept of standards is really a model that represents the person's purest invention of themselves in ways they choose to run their lives, without labels. That is it, in brief. The script they read from is their creation, no matter whether it has ever fit anyone else's before. It is not identification with a party or class; it is not confined to whether one is gay, lesbian, straight, agnostic, or religious. For instance, a well known pop singer with the reputation for exhibiting risqué behavior may adopt similar views socially and politically as a powerful respected politician, but it is also true that each one has distinctive approaches to standards, yet their standards remain high and in some cases new. One civil rights leader can have different views on how to handle civil rights issues than another, but it is certain that each fought similar injustices, while having a distinct approach to his standard.

Therefore, every personality accustom to superstardom brings with it some common thread they share and where they differ. In addition, those who discovered their unique standard came by it through self-knowledge. Some came by this self-knowledge instantaneously, and others took longer to identify it. They all, however, acquired it. In their own way, what many of these great talents left us with was more than their great works, but purpose.

One is reminded also of the many other superstar performers who come in the form of other professions, such as teachers, coaches, and mentors...people whose lives uniquely qualify them to be models, based on their character. Now, most would identify the quality of character as an element of standards. There is a tendency to hook it to the engine of standards. I believe there is some accuracy to this theory. Character, however, by definition is a trait, and one I sincerely believe is personality-based, or harnessed through the practice of good habits. Character is defined traditionally as whether a person is violent, or dishonest, and is directly associated with motive, trust, and integrity (other matrixes discussed in this book). However, one can have high and new standards but still lack character. Yet, one may ask, how can this be? The answer comes that in order for one to sustain the kind of standards required to become a true superstar performer, there must exist strong character. We all have heard of highly competitive people who win at almost everything, yet at any cost and enjoy the applause and praise of millions for it, but privately they fight significant character flaws, preventing them from entering the superstar performance class.

In any event, the standards discussed here require lots of risk-taking that in some cases has never been tried before, and will require strong character to accomplish. Having standards requires one to avoid others telling you what you should be or do, when your instincts hint at a greater vision. It is similar to the old tactics some children use when playing on a sandlot, by taunting their playmates to engage in activities they feel are of no value to them. This standard allows you to bridge your mind, heart, and soul into your greater good, and to trust those instincts.

One well known Public figure who grew-up in a foreign country, described two alternate worlds given to choose from: joining the Army, or working in the local factory. He was determined not to settle for the sedentary and mundane lifestyle that others in his village had chosen; he instinctually recognized that it was not for him. Determined to take a different route—he took authority over his destiny and dreamt of a different life that the villagers neither understood nor conceived. The dream, unbeknownst to them, was to one day become the best in his profession. Nothing could convince the non-believers that this vision was within his grasp. Go to America and do what? It was beyond their comprehension. Nevertheless, as serious skill trainers do, he dug in deep with relentless vigor and followed his heart. His secondary goal became his desire to live in the United States, live among the best at his profession, and meet his mentor. Even at this junction, one could envision him taking cues from his mentor, with the determination to succeed further than he did. This is a good example of one superstar performer learning from another.

Subsequently, his contribution would eclipse his mentor's in many ways by transcending the profession to a completely new standard, which even to this day reverberates amongst a generation of similar professionals.

One essential quality distinguishes him and continues to do so today, and it is his supreme confidence. His language is peppered with "I's," I am the best, I am going to be, and I am. These words indicate a distinct quality of standard-bearers, which separates them from others. They are constantly in tune with their specialness, and are confident in their choices. Therefore, it becomes less likely will we ever encounter a number of the unique greats that we encounter today in our lifetime. It is possible and probable, however, that we will see others who will come along and exceed their accomplishments or extend their standards.

Again, I must offer this note of disclosure: Achievement alone does not equate to superstardom, nor does it not mean one is void of the transgressions or weaknesses that all human beings face. This is not only a moral test I am describing. Though moral fortitude has never been a criterion for achievement, without moral fortitude—as emphasized before—I doubt anyone can maintain or achieve the level of standards contributing to real purpose. Moral fortitude provides a compass: a true north, signaling you are doing this not only for yourself, but for a higher calling beyond yourself, and undermining that calling somehow weakens your position.

I am also a true believer in acknowledging what one does in intimate gatherings gives some hints about their character and of what they stand for. A few questions may offer some insight:

How does a potential client spend their time outside their profession?

In what ways do they treat their friends and family?

What activities do they share with these friends and family members?

Are the activities they are involved in conducive to the person's mind, body, and soul?

How do clients deal with adversity?

I must mention one common thread found in the above suggestions and it is the quest for balance. Balance is important in all aspects pertaining to the overall strategies of the superstar performer and it most often comes from those individuals who fit well within the standards of the superstar. Later on in the book, we will examine how important the need is to have a strong and healthy cast of characters called your management team, which is essential in harnessing the vision of the super performer.

Matrix #2: Trust and Matrix #3: Integrity

TRUST

I have placed trust and integrity as second and third on the matrix tier, because they are the most fundamental to all successful relationships, including sustaining a long business tenure amongst partners. For when a manager-partner establishes a clear understanding of a client's vision and the big picture (of the working parts) of his and or standards, trust/integrity becomes the next step.

One common act of trust and integrity has been the handshake, used in most quarters as an acceptable contractual bid, equal in some cases to a written contract between persons, or to a person's word. All of these gestures have represented and have cemented deals in many agreements, even among high-level negotiators, all because the individuals involved trust each other.

I tend to believe the authentication of an agreement is born out of an intrinsic commitment where like values come together, though it can also arise in cases where values are different. The bottom line is that groups and individuals form partnerships because their trust is rooted in familiar interests and values. For example, I might have grown up in Hoboken, New Jersey where a set of values and rules was expected in the neighborhood. These values make up a part of the community's definition of integrity. But I do not believe anyone will dispute the claim that different communities still have the same basic definition of integrity, as it relates to the concept of trust. No matter how different the vernacular appears, everyone can conclude that it means the same thing to an Italian-American lad in Queens, New York as it does to a young lad in Savannah, Georgia.

What is different would perhaps be how persons and groups of people value trust. One can define it as a core of people or groups of communities making up their own rules and having the integrity to abide by them. If a client has given the authority to a friend to manage him or her, it often comes with the external and internal knowledge of having shared identical systems and rules of play. This is especially true if those friends grew up in the same environment for an extended period, and it holds even for those who are new acquaintances but who grew up in a similar community of rules.

Imagine that you are a super performer and you are introduced to a manager who grew up in X town, and you grew up in Y town, but in the same county—you may find that you both grew up in a thirty-mile radius of each other. You might even have shared experiences and events that you both were involved in. It might be that each one's high school played each other in football or basketball. It could mean, as well, that your high schools were rivals, something where your towns came together for an event. You may even have shared all these glorious memories, and know others in each other's communities, and yet not share the rules of that community or, for that matter, similarly value trust. You might be inclined to assume that if a person lives in proximity to my community; would they not share similar values and rules? This would make perfectly good sense. Yet, this is not always the case, because the person may not have experienced the ins and outs of convergences and what the relationship involves on a daily basis.

True friendships with deeper relationships require special responses different from the normal occasional acquaintances in passing—they require persons who value truthfulness and respect for one another, and who see eye to eye on certain shared concerns, visions—and yes, values. These elements measure up in defining aspects of integrity. Yet, no matter how talented a person might be, trust will always be first and foremost—the Holy Grail in building business and personal relationships. We have settled upon the fact that in spite of the many talents a performer may have, talent ranks sixth in importance on the matrix tier. The reason is that a client must first establish and maintain self-care routines to support self-mastery and discipline, prior to considering their talent.

Creating the proper and conducive environment for the superstar to thrive is the most worthy pursuit for anyone working with superstar performers. For example, there might come along an athlete in our time who may run faster than some of the fastest men alive, leap as high as never been done, and be as charming as the two mentioned. However, if he or she possesses dead-end value systems and dishonest traits, he or she has destroyed the key elements of a relationship, and none of the other abilities will matter much.

This is particularly true when the fiduciary care offered by accountants, lawyers, and some managers is of the type of trust that is technically legal. While every business and platonic relationship is a bargain—either for service for monetary gain, or bargaining for favors—it all serves a similar purpose. On the other hand, some relationships of trust—as we will be discussing later—pertain to intimate trust issues. In addition, this type of relationship bargaining is based upon friendship, where long-term knowledge of a person ranks superior to the accountant, or lawyer. Obviously, these intimate relationships are seen through the lens of knowledge of each other, and I am not suggesting here that a fiduciary relationship cannot be an intimate one. However, some would require the need for a person to walk in that person's shoes, to know or at least become empathetic to the person's world—or even if you cannot imagine that, try using reality therapy to show you understand them.

Many long-term pairings starting as fiduciary relationships have ended up becoming intimate circle relationships of trust. It makes the situation easier if long-term friends come equipped with the tools to support their client friends. For instance, several high regarded athletes' recently released members of their management team in exchange for close friends whom they have known their entire lifetime. These particular friends, assigned to take care of their other businesses aside from their athletic interests, knew those performers inside out. In this situation, one can only make the assumption that they chose these friends because they deeply understood their superstar performers and their brand, and emphatically trusted each other. One could also believe that this trust, being tested many times, and without hesitation, encouraged them to instinctively roll the dice by entrusting them with their business affairs. These superstar friends knew their strengths, and weaknesses, and could size up where they best fit within their organization. But I also believe their most invaluable contribution to those athletes' came from time to time in being simply their friend.

INTEGRITY

Integrity is not a concept one can easily define, but similar to Justice Harlan's statement on obscenity, one may not know what it is, but one knows it when one sees it. Likewise, integrity is a concept that one may not know what it is, but knows it when one sees it. I believe that integrity encompasses aspects of honesty and truthfulness, but it is also much broader than that. Integrity, in my mind—and perhaps others' minds—determines how consistent a person's actions are on a balanced approach on a number of fronts. We cannot always expect to uphold the highest level of integrity, all the time. Even highly effective and superstar performers do not always uphold it at its highest level, but when integrity is called upon, they do rise to the occasion. While individuals may fall short of their own value system from time to time, in no way does this indicate hypocrisy. Besides, superstar performers are aware of their weaknesses and vulnerabilities and are willing to work on them because they believe not doing so would impede their natural progress. And so, not living up to one's natural progress prevents him from living up to and honoring the purest self.

For example, let's say my friend was confronted with a known adversary, and he approached him to fight. If you were a true-blue friend, you would stand with him. If you guys were outnumbered, by two to six, then you both would be fighting for your lives. You would then find yourself fighting for yourself instead for the other person, because your survival mechanism would kick in. In fact, you might forget about the other person and say, "Every man for himself." On the other hand, the rules of the community and its ecosystem of values may have dictated that you be your brother's keeper, and exercise a code of chivalry. One might believe that the qualities and definitions of character would be the same across all value-driven communities, but this is not the case. For many, and in some ecosystems, character isn't proven by whether you will throw yourself in front of a train to save someone, but by events that can test your stress level and tolerance for adversity—which are major components of integrity if you are in crisis management mode.

What it often tests is a level of courage. In a management position, courage may have nothing to do with physical feats; it may be as simple as defying the rules of the tribe for the client's greater good, and instead of being a yes-man, telling the superstar performer that a decision will be detrimental to his or her career. The need for this kind of "in your face" attitude is perhaps the reason why many superstars elect their friends as managers. These relationships have forged particular expectations governed by the rules of the environment, and have rested their fate on each person's knowledge of the other.

Conversely, the new suits ("suits" reference corporate types that give professional advice without any personal attachment) who come along might not have this advantage. They start from the bottom in this respect, even if they have excellent technical skills, but they can quickly overcome this deficit of personal rapport through the process of goodwill and good faith found in similar consistent core values.

Here is a point I have made in these pages many times with one simple example. I grew up in a rural town, and like most small towns, certain distinct qualities defined my town: courtesy, basic honesty, and one golden rule, "Do unto others as you would have them to do unto you." This mantra is more often the rule than the exception, and it was tested on the day I lost my checkbook.

After having visited a grocery store one day, I left only to discover later that my checkbook was missing. In a moment of panic, I returned to the store and inquired about it, to no avail—I had no luck.

My anxiety reached fever pitch, and I couldn't stop worrying about where my checks might be. I returned home, and a few moments later, I received a telephone call from my clergyman. He told me that a colleague of his had found my checkbook, and noticed I had given a contribution to the church. By this kind gesture, I was able to make connections with the individual and receive my checkbook. It immediately became clear to me that this person lived the identical value system I was accustomed to, and it's clear that had my checkbook been picked up by somebody with the opposite value system, this situation would have had a much different outcome. It goes to show, it all comes down to whose rulebook is being played.

One other point to make is that sometimes opposites attract in business situations. Clients are drawn to individuals who hold strengths they lack. Let's see—it is easy to determine that when we lack skills in accounting, we should hire someone with those skills; or for legal matters, one hires a competent attorney. Then again, it is uncommon for us to hire individuals who hold interpersonal skills we lack. Yet, when we hire individuals who hold these skills, and personal integrated value systems we lack, we have leapt to another place in our growth that serves our better interest. For it takes a great deal of courage to acknowledge weaknesses, but admitting them displays a part of our integrity that seeks growth beyond our comfort zone. Moreover, while it feels good to surround ourselves with individuals to shoot the breeze with, they are in essence less inclined to add to our growth, especially if they are not willing to grow along with us.

The bottom line in many business relationships—and in personal relationships—remains: Whom do you trust? Who chimes in and gets you on all aspects of your career, in not only your business affairs, but also your life? And if you must peel the layers back to determine who holds authentic values, realistically, I guess, it is hard to emphatically trust anyone. In any case, it may come down to you deciding to deal with the devil you know, rather than the one you don't know.

Matrix #4: Preparation

I remember, in excruciating detail, working on the roof of my parents' house, replacing old shingles with new ones. Tearing the heavy black tar-like material from the roof was the hardest work I have ever encountered. Today I can still smell the stench of the tar and the sensation that occurred of the draining, drugged feeling that eclipsed my seven-year-old body on a hot August day. When I collapsed from the heat, I swore I would never do this again.

Later on I had to eat my words and retract that statement, since subsequently I found myself, again, thrust into similar situations, time after time—raking yards with Mr. X, picking up cans on weekends with Mr. Y, and raking my parents' yard—all three acres of it—for the sake of developing stamina for future work. I left, however, not minding the heat or the back-breaking work I once dreaded. I was ready to take on any challenge that faced me, but only because these experiences helped prepare me for other experiences. Moreover, as you will discover in the following pages, many more have done the same.

The irony of it all is that the conditioning that most athletes endure is no more rigorous than the ordeals of mind and body required to become truly proficient in any profession. The difficulties of preparation are the same across the board. A writer, for instance, who writes habitually for several hours a day, holds to the same endurance ritual as that of an athlete who plans and participates in a game. Writing, for what seem to be long endless hours, has in it similar conditioning as the long practices endured by athletes, all in an effort to discipline their minds and bodies. When one great coach conducted practices with his team, he conditioned them—as many coaches do today with their players—to endure the stresses of the game. While he became notorious for conducting two-hour practice drills, he was both strategic and tactical in realizing the effects those drills had on not only the players' physical being, but their emotional, psychological, and mental state as well. These exercises, he believed, contributed to keeping an edge over other teams who dominated in size, but were lacking in conditioning.

So, I truly believe those earlier experiences of my childhood—hauling shingles off my parents' house, raking yards, and other physical labor—had a profound effect on conditioning and preparing me for other equally challenging tasks. I am also convinced, as well, that Alexander Graham Bell's love and thirst for learning contributed to his spending hour upon hour in serious study, and prepared him for the long and arduous process of his eventual invention.

The activities we subject ourselves to, what appear as meandering steps, are woven into a fabric comprised of purposeful plans and activities directed toward reaching an ultimate goal. Preparation becomes an exercise of both internal endurance and self-satisfaction of personal conditioning. With that in mind, one must understand that preparation not only fosters skill training, but also fosters emotional and psychological conditioning. This is a concept never lost by many highly effective and superstar performers, but grounded in well-researched doctrines of the ages. Furthermore, you will find comfort as you read the chapter pertaining to the matrix on talent and find that superstar performers adhere to rigorous preparation. Though they all appreciated and recognized the beauty of their gifts, ultimately the journey proved more rewarding. And while preparation involves much the same factors described above, it must be grounded in effective tools. As one will find, harnessing talent does not just happen; it occurs when a performer has created the proper habits for it to grow.

Preparation, as well, is connected to the previous matrixes that have been discussed, and the ones that follow. Establishing standards is a self-discipline tool that is necessary in order for the other matrixes to thrive. Trust and integrity become part of the engine, requiring the superstar performer to employ honest hard work to his or her pursuit. In the end, preparation is as much about living up to those standards as anything else, and feeds one's internal drive in deciding whether their contribution will simply be good work, or masterful work.

Yet no matter how talented you are, the effort still requires steadfastness, consistency, and hard work. Therefore, in the vernacular of the superstars, seldom will you hear them use the terms "struggle," or "can't do"—most will refer to their dilemma as an "opportunity"—but word usage has limitless capacity. Found interwoven in this language are threads of conditioning principles used all the time in their preparation and everyday schemes, rewarding them by breathing life into their pursuits.

Superstar performers, if anything, are thrifty, focused, keen on seizing opportunity, staying in their lane, and seeking knowledge. If anyone tells you that superstar performing is comprised of individuals clawing at each other and venting out a few expletives for shock value as preparation, they are deceiving themselves. The preparation they undergo is an audacious, lonesome, and sometimes boring undertaking with no cheering fans or high-fives. These accolades come—if they ever do—after long successive failures on their way to becoming great.

Fred in a Box

Anyone who has ever pursued a professional degree, either as a doctor or lawyer, will attest to the challenges you go through in balancing your life between study time and other parts of your life. I went through a similar exercise when I was balancing work and attending law school. I drew a line in the sand by asking myself, "What are the *intentions* of my goal?" The profundity of this nagging question further drove me in searching for a number of answers: Why did I want to spend three—actually four—years in what could be considered a marathon, studying a taxing profession? When those questions were finally answered, I was ready to prepare for the task. I say *prepare*. For it was as much about emotional, mental, and physical preparation as any other task, but it was also, notably, about correct habit-forming.

Therefore, in order to ensure my success, I began my journey by listing all the activities I saw as pertinent, deciding upon the ones that were important to me, and managing to reduce my decision down to four categories: my health, family, personal life, and spiritual life. Anything else remained secondary. When asked by my fiancée one day how my schedule looked in a typical week, and I showed her my schedule, her response was "You don't have a life," and my reply to her was "Yes, you're right, because I live in a box." The preparation game in my case centered on the basic philosophy of "Keep it simple, stupid." The strategies and tactics I used proved vital to my success, in that I was reduced to focusing on particular areas suitable to my needs, which happened to require me to "live in a box." The box included work, workouts, school, study, and home. My life therefore became work, workout, school, study and home. This was my box, but within that box, I gave myself room to attend to my family needs, and replenish my soul with daily spiritual meditation and reflection. Thus, the exercise never entirely became a dull or wrenching under-taking, though it was not easy. There was always some form of prepa-ration going on.

This type of routine might not work for everyone, but for others, such as myself, the rigid approach insulated me, in a sense, protecting me against distractions. Someone has to be serious about their craft in order to think of unorthodox or drastic measures to accomplish their goal. Yet the nuances of accomplishing this feat require steps similar to those that superstar performers use in order to reach their goals. As Plato once wrote, "The first and best victory is for a man to conquer himself." By controlling oneself—including one's emotions—one controls his or her destiny. So therefore, throughout this book, the real emphasis on preparation is twofold: personal preparation of oneself, and mastery of the craft.

Matrix #5: Passion

Like many terms that have been discussed in this writing, passion is complex and complicated, and its various meanings and implications could fill several books. Lust is one synonym for passion, which creates a strong response and leads in many directions. The Greeks and the Romans spoke almost excessively of passion and were driven by it in their activities. The Roman general Mark Anthony fought and won battles with it, and because of his tempestuous personality and uncompromising demeanor, he suffered his greatest defeat because of it.

In both instances, passion was displayed as a dangerous, necessary, and yet powerful force, manifesting itself to be either for good or evil. Depending on how one uses passion, it can be a blessing or a curse. In any event, most will agree that having passion is an essential part of superstar performing. However, what does it mean in the frame of reference to the superstar performer pertaining to passion? In the simplest language, it means "desire and it is not a desire of sprints or yards, but one of miles.

The desire I am referencing is the desire to manifest in unselfish terms, ascending to a grander vision other than self. The noticeable difference, however, of a superstar's desire, relative to that of a regular Joe, is based entirely on the mastery of its intensity. One of the reasons why this may be the case is due in part to the average man's lack of ability to understand the demarcation between good passion and bad, and how one or the other is properly conditioned.

This statement cannot be overlooked, for many have mistakenly believed that unbridled youthful passion is equivalent to mature steady passion, and because this assumption has been believed as fact, it has confused the concept of desire. Considering the outlandish and over-the-top behavior we have witnessed among some people today, it is easy to see the two passions as similar.

The passion shown by superstar performers is determined by their attitude and altitude. In other words, as soon as they are able to recognize their personal powers, they are better able to gauge their internal rumblings and silence, and wisely channel them. One way they reserve those energies comes in the form of picking their fights at the appropriate time, choosing mountains over molehills, and defending activities necessary to protect their mission and vision. Furthermore, these superstar performers were also more than willing to leave lesser activities and goals in the hands of non-skill trainers, because they realized those activities to be insignificant.

Moreover, superstar performers have trained themselves to avoid the nuisance of noise by preserving their passion for important matters, which prevents them from being distracted. This training is essential in their development because it allows the performer to spend less time finding fault with others, and more time perfecting their imperfections. This, in itself, takes a tremendous amount of discipline and practice. I emphasis practice because the carefree, unbridled, narcissistic, and reckless display of some individuals we have come to identify as superstars represents misguided passion. Their outside appearance provides a smokescreen for comic relief; while this may be entertaining, underneath their exterior, they cry out in search of ways to connect their heart, mind, and soul to a purpose. Even if these individuals are seen as having authentic talent, they soon lose any self-respect and cannot be taken seriously.

Then again, we all have known many talented individuals who lost their passion and were able to regain their footing in a spectacular way! Many are familiar with talented actors and actresses, who started their careers with an unselfish intent to do well with their abilities, but lost the passion that others have come to see them. Yes, they are able to perform their talent well, but it lacked the special zing it had before. Due in part to drug use, selfish actions, and self-loathing, they were destroying themselves and on the verge of torpedoing their careers. However, in spite those indiscretions, there are people who still believed in their talent, and an industry that continued to reward them with film roles, in lieu of their many arrest.

What occurs in many of these situations results in the news media and tabloids chronicling every move of their lives and the twist and turns of it. It furthermore adds fodder to the circus that is going on in their lives and adds also amusing commentary to what appears as a train wreck happening in living color. For many, they were playing in their own movie, but this was real life. Here, truth is better than fiction, cloaked in retakes, outtakes, and well-edited film footage.

What the outside world often don't see are the private breakdowns, as it isn't possible to know what is going on inside a person during these challenging times. Although it is possible for anyone to produce successful work during tumultuous times, true success, I remind you, is found when life has balance. Yet still, it is possible for anyone and anything to rise again. After many years being tired of being tired, a person can be vindicated and, usher in passionate productive work, suitable to their acting talent and renewed passion. It all goes to show that we can all fall down, but we also can get up.

In a tale of art imitating life, the contradictions of the human experience offer us more than enough examples of lost passion once again found. In many talented people's situations, their talent never left them, but the resurgence of their passion to serve again, and share their talent with others found new life. Of course, what happens is a mature, responsible, accepting and humble person emerges with new wings to fly.

The expansion of passion gained in the situation prescribed elevates a more enriched life that could never be envisioned before the ravaging toll drugs and other trappings took on their lives, and which dispersed their energies to nowhere.

While it is true that Thomas Edison summoned these same

emotions thousands of times, as does the terrific inventors we have today, and others to come. What was so transformative about their passion, and especially the experience of renewed of others a like, was that they were not insular. They were not confined to their own unselfish acts. They instead *expanded* to include others in the sphere of their vision, which served everyone. Furthermore, whenever they saw something in the world requiring fixing, room was made for their gifts in pursuing those solutions.

Take for example; the sixties became a nesting ground for social activism and change and for those who hunger for it. Like today, the unusual degrees of issues inspired ordinary individuals to do extraordinary things in expanding their passion.

The civil rights movement galvanized a wealth of individuals from all races, classes, and, social and economic status. It aroused the passions in college students, professors, celebrities, and political leaders to join the movement in one single passion, to eradicate injustices every where. The movement inspired a number of maverick lawyers to take on the system and challenge it for many of its wrongs.

Many of these brave young black lawyers directed their passion toward the plight of poor children any where they could be found. They dug deep into the lives of these children who suffered the most in the United States, engrossed in knowing almost everything there was to know about the profound effects that poverty had on those lives. They dedicated their lives to that single quest to eradicate it. They even ignited the passion of a young lawyer who would become one of the most powerful leaders in the world to join the cause. As with many others whose inner being longs for a specific calling in the world, these young professionals found theirs when they saw and faced the devastating poverty that existed in many poverty-stricken areas at the height of the civil rights movement.

Every aspect of their being was permeated with a calling to help children and to expand their talents and efforts for their cause—but also, this work gave them a higher level of satisfaction that they felt they would never receive anywhere else. When superstar performers such as those young lawyers exercise their *embryonic freedom* in the way they demonstrated, powerful things in the universe take place. Fewer disturbances clog the interstate of less-important pursuits, because one acknowledges an authentic intrinsic motive at play.

The chapter that follows this one is on talent, and it examines it on a spectrum. Why talent is placed as number six on the matrix, rather than at a higher order than the ones we have noted, has a lot to do with establishing a foundation for talent to stand on. My observation leads me to conclude that standards, integrity, trust, preparation, and passion are the necessary legs for that stool. Talent will have a difficult time maintaining itself if it lacks the proper footing. Though talent represents the crown jewel of the individual, that jewel, from time to time, requires polishing.

Matrix #6: Talent

Since talent is the ultimate crown jewel of a superstar performer, one might assume it should be placed higher on the matrix tier. However, as the previous chapters have suggested, talent alone does not itself make a superstar performer complete. In support of this theory, one can name a number of super-performers whose demise came due to their own careless, burnt-out, and drugged-out lives. Events in the media bear this out, showing well-known people falling over themselves in utter embarrassment.

I personally have witnessed this unkind, merciless, and painful reality of seeing many talented homeless persons living in trash on the sidewalks and in the garden spots outside the city hall in a major metropolitan city. Among these individuals were well-educated, highly trained, and talented people—but due to a twist of bad luck, they ended in a mire of circumstances that any one of us might have been subjected to: divorce, tragedy, addiction, misfortune, and other issues unresolved. No one can figure out whether any of those individuals had families or loved ones who cared for them, or if addicted habits were the cause of their downfall. It is fair to say that in spite of the enormous talents these people had, they more than likely would not have sustained themselves without support.

On the other hand, it may be true that others who have genuine talent and support might sometimes take their talent for granted and think they need only to rest on their laurels to succeed. In this situation, there is the tendency to coast in getting through the next project meeting, audition, exam, etc., but these successes may ring hollow. With or without support, there is definitely abuse of their gifts, for lack of a better word, and a lazy attitude toward improving upon them. No matter how talented a person might be care in improving that talent is necessary.

Even one great twentieth century artist acknowledged that his fleeting talent as a prodigy would have been insignificant had he not improved upon it. He recognized his prodigious talent early, but was keenly aware that in order to perfect his talent of those before, would take a lifetime; referring to his eventual mature painting. In fact, it was indeed his deliberate practice that helped produced his amazing work after his many hours of focused work. It is clear, however, that his earlier aptitude helped to spring his successes; it is unclear whether he would have accomplished his successes without instruction and guidance from teachers or mentors. This then leads one to ask the question: To what extent is guidance needed to harness true talent? Many believe deliberately designed exercises are essential to super-performers' success. This premise is based on performers receiving early instructions from teachers, guiding students in correct exercises and discipline for improving specific skills.

This is no different from a football coach who coaches a player on how to properly block, run routes, or catch a ball. The apparent difficulty of superstar performers becoming great without instruction is not unnoticed. Superstar performers require practice, day in and day out, working through various integrated skill training mechanics in order to reach a particular level. Gifted musicians can master musical scales, but understanding the variances of combinations of those scales requires creativity, intense teaching, and guidance in correction. The actor who attends workshops gains invaluable lessons on whether the techniques he has gained are proper for acting coaches in gauging acting cues. The business mogul, having received general knowledge of business theories, will have mastered them well enough to the point where he has creatively invented his own rules of business transactions. Moreover, it might be determined in these cases that earlier mentoring by someone else helped forge the curiosity to extend this knowledge.

One important point here is that a superstar performer, in general, narrows their skills down to one specific accomplished skill. For while a few performers have succeeded in multi-tasking additional skills well, of those skills, I am certain in saying they are supreme in only one. The thought of mastering one field in a lifetime is difficult enough, unless you are a Da Vinci, and the last I checked, there does not appear to be many of them around.

Furthermore, the task of becoming a superstar performer is not an easy proposition, but it is possible, which explains why so few accomplish it. In my opinion, unless a performer has solidified the five other matrixes earlier mentioned and the remaining two that follow, he or she will have a difficult time in reaching his or her highest performance goals.

So the question becomes: What does it take, talent-wise, to become a superstar performer? Well, one would think it takes at least general intelligence. Yet, being simply talented or intelligent does not guarantee superstardom—but not having either quality certainly won't produce a superstar. In contrast, many other theories produce a variety of definitions and forms of intelligence, but for the most part, we will stick with the nonprofessional's understanding of intelligence in association to talent, to explain and discuss it.

In *Talent Is Overrated*, Geoff Colvin relates an experiment conducted by a group of researchers in England on the concept of talent. He emphasized much practice as the metrics for super performance. If you have the chance in reading the experiment, it will become easy to determine where the logic of this experiment is going, but it is undetermined whether the big issue of innate ability finds people wired for a particular skill. For instance, when one great captain of industry points-out that he was hardwired at birth to allocate capital and cultivate the ability to spot winning investments, one has to think, what does that mean in tangible terms? Can we not say that undeveloped talent might be lost if it is not trained or discovered? Does it mean he had developed something that is already available to all, or was it dependent on conditioning through various training mechanisms? These are legitimate questions to ponder.

Perhaps his initial activities instinctively lend him to various exercises or activities that he was naturally prone to. Yes, maybe that is the key in his case. Even if we were to take this position, we then might take the same view, let's say...about an NBA player, who by many standards was not as athletic as a others, yet there is no question that he is considered as great as they are. But was he hard-wired for it? A better explanation may conclude that certain natural skills that some have can be transferable to a number of occupations. This person's general intelligence and his prodigious hard work were well-known to his teammates and opponents. His preparation was noticeable by the likes of the other great ones. If any of these men were unconvinced of the extent of his preparation, they soon were made aware of it by his ability to change a game in minutes.

Nothing guaranteed his abilities and successes in basketball, but he took his personal skills and made them work for him. There is, however, one possibility that may account for his success, and that may be that picking up a basketball in his state is embedded in the DNA of its youngsters who grow up there, as automatic as breathing. Understanding those kinds of environments, and the conditioning they offer, helps in contributing to the person's skill training, and determines their acceleration rate. Nevertheless, it will always be about conditioning when it comes to developing talent. Without conditioning, a gifted talented person stays a regular talented person.

What if a great NBA player, in lieu of exploring his enormous gifts, hadn't committed the time and effort by stretching himself in practicing after games to improve his skills, or what if he hadn't developed the grueling off-season drills he became known for? Would he have become the great legend he has become? If a great golf coach had not conditioned a great golfer's mind to avoid the needless distractions that occurred once he faced the whispers and sounds from the gallery, he might not have developed a steel-trap mind. If both men, with their exceptional innate abilities, had relied on talent, they would never have reached their highest level.

Nor can one discredit earlier exposure—no matter how unorthodox it seems—to particular skills as irrelevant.

In the end it very well might have been these competitors fierce practicing and conditioning that made them into world champions, but we can make no mistake about the early conditioning affecting their cognitive aptitude, and the impact it had on the way they think and react to situations today. The same goes for the actor who rehearses a part over and over, who has demonstrated the many layers of conditioning necessary to reach maximum potential.

I do want to make this point before I go on; I do not want anyone to misinterpret my sentiment regarding talent, nor get the idea that I devalue it as unimportant, when in fact, superstar performers are unable to become superstar performers without general abilities. Whether they started out with mediocre talent to begin with, or just a hint of it, there has to be some ability there. I do, however, believe that many unlikely winners, whom others believed to be "diamonds in the rough," are superstar performers based upon some special quality that initial observation failed to identify. On the other hand, closer observation of these talented people can also reveal their special aptitudes. What becomes unavailing to many actually reveals their true calling. Furthermore, when they identified their special gifts, they began the necessary deliberate practice essential to achieve their greatness:

Bodybuilders trained thousands of hours with grueling workouts to achieve their near perfect bodies. Many budding national television hosts perfect their interviewing skills by practicing them at a local television station and those who chose the service of peace practice civil disobedience by conditioning their lives to meditate and private study. They were all exposed to the need to practice.

The IQ vs. EQ Factor

Two concepts come to mind when considering ability: intelligence quotient and emotional quotient. Whether you are an advocate of one or the other is less important than how the two reconcile themselves. I won't go into a great deal of detail on this subject, because it would take volumes to understand. Besides, it is not necessary here in order to make my point. It is, however, important in sizing up which of these models is the more important to our superstar performers. Nevertheless, sound reasoning suggests that superstar performers have at least general intelligence. This, I believe, we can agree on. If you are of the persuasion supporting Wechsler IQ theories, then this might be where your thoughts reside. If you subscribe more to the emotional quotient theories, you will be an advocate of multiple intelligence theory.

Since the discussion of this book pertains to a score of specific fields relating to variable mechanics regarding intelligence, one can rest upon general intelligence as the starting point. It has become accepted that even an idiot savant, though lacking in other skills, can demonstrate spectacular prodigy math skills, but still may have trouble accomplishing simple matters such as tying his shoelaces, a task that the average four-year-old can accomplish. Why this is the case becomes unclear and open for speculation. If a person is a talented musician, can he not be, as well, an talented accountant, if it is discovered he cognitively thinks equally well, left and right? Of course, he can, but this rarely occurs.

Simply, a left-brain person tends to be analytical, whereas a right-brain person is interpreted as being more instinctive and creative. One United States President—a left-hander—is said to be methodical and analytic in his approach; he may not be a talented artist. The other, although he thinks out his plans, can be known to act from his gut, delivering what most understand as an instinctual approach, but no one knows if he can "play a banjo on his knee." The theories cross paths sometimes in many ways. I've known judges who have professed to be terrible at math, yet if you look at the skills applicable to great lawyers, it is as closely aligned as any profession to playing chess, which is an activity associated with calculus. Moreover, as one continues to investigate profession after profession, you will discover that there is an interweaving of both, though one tends to dominate.

This thinking is fascinating on a number of fronts when it comes to activities, by informing us that we have a proclivity toward our natural skills and a hint of instinctive ability. If this is the case, the question most pressing here becomes: Does instinct resides in the emotional side of our psyche, or in the intellectual mechanics of logic and memory of our brain, and if so, does it affect our reasoning? The Greeks believed in rational thought as incomplete without the support of intuition, and therefore considered rational thought a separate entity from the mystical intuition, or "gut feeling."

All of us have experienced the sudden thought of a person coming to our mind and moments later the person appears or calls. What if the stockbroker picked a stock based on a feeling or an arthritic arm, and it proved to be correct? Would the process be odd? I know someone is thinking right now, "This sounds close to a psychic reading." I assume in some corners it could be interpreted that way. However, would it sound unreasonable if I told you that a number of highly sophisticated stock pickers have relied on methods of this nature to pick a stock? Is the process a logical one in their toolbox in performing their work? Would they be considered less crazy in a highly technical field, relying upon math, numbers, and flow charts in making decisions, if they dabbled in some old-fashioned psychic mumbo-jumbo once in a while? The conclusion I came to in considering both choices of abilities is that talent and intelligence have multiple dimensions of equally important weight. Certainly, superstar performers have become masters of manipulating both. What it has done is mesh the theories of general intelligence enthusiasts, emotional quotient enthusiasts, and those who rely on instinctive perception, all into one.

There are some well known entrepreneurs who cite their use, sometimes, of their sixth sense—what feels right—in making decisions. In no way do they ignore research, but numbers play a less-reliable role in telling the whole story. You will be pleased to find that superstar performers masterfully balance intelligence, special talent, and a keen instinctive perception of their abilities with natural ease.

Matrix #7: Support System

Now that I have gone through six matrixes of importance to the success of a superstar performer, we come to what I consider the most important matrix of them all: the support system. You might have noticed that the six prior matrixes dealt strictly with the performer's self-awareness; the performer being in tune with their special talents or lack thereof, and the *inner* qualities necessary to build on them. Those matrixes are evaluations of the person's *self* and their authentic true north—the performer as the captain of his ship who will navigate his career, where others have accepted the call to support his or her efforts.

Furthermore, if there is one chapter that needs your greatest attention, please give it to this one. For if ever a performer is to become a true superstar, having a strong support system is crucial. These supports are as numerous as the day is long, from immediate relatives to the one-time piano teacher who taught you for years, or even the person you met further along in your career. They all bear importance in the lives of superstar performers. Nevertheless, there are different levels of support systems to consider, and distinguishing among them is as significant in shaping the life and career of the performer as anything. One support system is close friends, family members, and others alike. Another support system consists of staffers who are hired people to follow the wishes of the superstar's organization. Then there are the contract players who work outside the organization, but are less intimately associated with the superstars. All of these positions are essential personnel as support for the performer. However, certain positions are deemed "disconnectors"—people who strictly associate themselves for business purposes only—while others are "connectors," whose interest is intimate and personal. While they are all part of the support system, the significance of each moves along different quadrants based on different intent, task, functions, motivations, and principles. In this kind of system, some support systems may collapse and the performer will still go on, but in one set of systems, if they collapse, it will cause a domino effect that will greatly affect the performer.

In our discussion, here, we will use the following terms: fix-its, prevent-its, connectors, disconnectors, system of care, intimate circle, associates circle, independent contractors, and go-fers, in order to lay the framework of the quadrants. Each one of these terms are important in understanding the larger picture of team management and propelling our thinking to see where persons in different roles fit in, and where they are least helpful and where they are the most useful. Further, keep in mind that all roles have their importance in terms of shaping the person or shaping the person as the brand. As one will notice in Figure 1, there are four squares:

Personal Management Matrix

Inside Circle

Intimate Circle	Associates Circle
Prevent-its	Fix-its
"Connectors"	"Connectors"
Examples	Examples
• Family	• Attorney
• Boyhood Friends	• Business Managers
• Personal Managers	• Accountants
• Business Partners	• Podiatrists
• Psychologist	• Surgeons

• Therapist	• Doctors
• Spiritual Advisors	• Crisis Managers

Outside Circle

Independent Contractors	Go-fers / Servicing
Non-Connectors	Non-Connectors
Disconnectors	Disconnectors to the vision

Examples	Examples
• Rack Jobbers (stacking records in a store)	• Proctor & Gamble
• Promoters (promoting a product)	
• Producers	• FedEx
• Engineers	• Sam Goody's
• Theaters	• Coca-Cola
• Movie Houses	• Sprint
• Stage Crew	• Connected to the product,
	• not the vision.

The top of Quadrants I and II is labeled Inner Circle; here, one will see that Quadrant I is labeled Intimate Circle, and in that box you see the terms prevent-its, connectors, and fix-its. These individuals' focus is on personal management. Quadrant II is labeled Associates Circle, and it too is labeled as a connector, but these individuals are fix-its, and they focus more or less on crisis management issues. The bottom half of the quadrants is labeled as the Interdependent Circle and it are Quadrants III and IV. Quadrant III is labeled Independent Contractors, who are disconnectors; Quadrant IV are go-fers, and they too are considered disconnectors. Each one of these individuals plays important roles in the life of the superstar performer. As you may have noticed, the terms appear self-explanatory, but their integrations are unusually interwoven in a manner where the terms can be misleading. The quadrants examine those personalities who fit under each category. But in order to further clarify, I will take each quadrant and go through them to show the distinction. I will address each in reverse order of closeness to the performer:

Go-fers: Although the term describes a person who works as an employee in terms of running errands for an employer, here the term is inverted to mean the opposite. Go-fers are the employers who represent delivery service to the superstar performer, but these delivery services are behemoth institutions that everyone has typically used from time to time. They include such giant brand institutions as Costco to Coco-Cola, whom others seek attachment to because they provide a high delivery of services for a superstar performer. However, they have no mental or spiritual connection to the superstar performer, and hold the least management role as it comes to the performer's understanding of his vision, career, desires, and mission. On one hand, you may ask, "How can a concept be both less important to a person and most powerful entity to it at the same time?" Well, in our concept here, they are, in the simplest sense, only there to sell something; a bargaining for exchange for work done…they receive payment, and they're gone. In this case, the go-fers view their relationship to the superstar performer with the attitude, "They can take what we can give, or leave it." In terms of advantage, you play their game or you don't play at all, because they feel as though they have the upper hand in negotiation. They also can choose from a cast of thousands to do business with, knowing others will line up to do business with them no matter what.

Examples of go-fers are manufactures, suppliers, retail stores, or makers of goods. For a business enterprise, it might mean paper supply companies, or office supply companies. They could even have a long-standing relationship with these companies, but remain disconnectors in the overall system of care strategies of the performer. In a few cases, however, there are enterprises that are smaller go-fers that depend upon superstar performers in selling their products by giving added attention to their product or brand. These relationships pose a close stake, and may have built a bond fitting for their arrangement. But I am still of the belief that companies act on general vital interest for their good, while not having any problems in going to the next pitch man if difficulty arises. In other words, these smaller go-fers still remain disconnectors, but in the interdependent circle. Here are lists of a few go-fers:

- Proctor & Gamble
- Johnson & Johnson
- Apple Computer
- Caramel Theaters
- Candace's
- Gatorade
- Dell Computer
- AT&T

Independent Contractor: Independent contractors are a step up above the food chain of a go-fer, but only in a few respects. They tend to be the persons who do a great deal of the ground work, bequeathed by the inner circle crew, who are connectors. They are disconnectors, considered as work-for-hire Trojans, holding insignificant input in the shaping of the vision of the performer, but significant in carrying out duties for them. Their primary function, although a service, is one whereby they have an inside understanding of the working of the brand of the performer, but do not participate in every day planning. Their responsibility is similar to that of a promoter who promotes a record, or a product; the field operator of a retail store; the record jobber in a music retail store, or the buyer of fashion line; a theater operator who provides the hall for the performer. Any and all of these references are defined—in the context of our discussion—as independent contractors, because they are essential in certain deliveries of service for the performer to present his or her brand.

Independent contractors are all around us and they are important to the performer's future projects. Relationships are built of these unions, sometimes similar to those of the connectors. Program directors have been close friends to musicians. Entertainment news reporters have been close friends to actors and actresses. Therefore, it is possible that these kinds of unions can represent business associations.

The Inner Circle

Quadrants I & II are of greater importance in management in the performer's life, and their nay or yea rules the day. They focus on two matters: improving and preserving the performer's vision, and preventing damage to it. They are connectors who act as windows into the world of the performer, and if there is any group of people who will sing the praises and correct the wrongs of the performer, it will be these individuals.

The Associates Circle: Quadrant II is part of the Inner Circle and generally are skill trainers who are there to be "fix-its." They come in the form of accountants, attorneys, public relations representatives, business managers, and other professionals whose skills are specifically designed for the performer's business structure. They come with an objective point of view, calling it as they see it. Their aims are as crisis managers, providing instant professional service, and they are less particular about holding hands. Nevertheless, they cement a natural propensity to interweave their duties and job description by accenting it with emphatic response. Because they are vital to the personal care of the performer and are a major part of their inner circle, they are well within the circle as a connector. Accountants are essential to a performer in order to budget their monies. They also are advisers on tax issues when it comes to the internal revenue service. Attorneys, of course, provide legal advice on matters that are civil and criminal; the business managers negotiate potential deals in line with opportunities centered on the manifest function of the performer, and pertain to the overall vision. The opportunities that managers secure might provide additional capital for future business deals, but well within the intentions and purpose of the performer. Public relations gurus speak or write the words conveying the feelings and thoughts of the person to the world; the mouthpiece on new, old, or unchanged conditions in their approach.

These groups of people are part of one-half of the team management group that offers the kind of system of care required for crisis engagement. They can also be—as we will be discussing soon—closely associated with the intimate circle. Yet what differs slightly is whether the associates circle has made enough emotional deposits to be considered grouped with the intimate circle. When I earlier mentioned how some professional athletes chose close friends to operate their certain businesses, those choices were based not only on the earlier emotional deposits made in their lives, but perhaps on certain qualities they saw essential to their business successes.

Note: it is important to understand that though generally associates circles aren't required to understand the vision of the performer, their thinking is based on objectivity: the law, the math, and the message are most important to them in black and white. Their tools do not have to fit into anyone's vision or plan, unless they are already members of the intimate circle. Now, "inner circles" are not the same as "intimate circles." The terms sound interchangeable, but although the "intimate circle" and the "associates circle" are under the same tent of the inner circle, their roles are different. The intent of each can be different. You notice I said *can* be different, because at certain junctions their roles can easily switch in a blink of an eye. What bridges the two is the trust and integrity barrier that we have discussed earlier. In any event, "intimate circle" folks are essential to the emotional, mental, physical and spiritual life of the performer.

The Intimate Circle: (Quadrant I) The intimate circle is comprised of persons who are the holy grail of the team management system. They are connectors and the caretakers of the jewel, meaning the performer. If there is any group of people who represents the example of a "system of care" service, it is these people. Unlike the associates, who are fix-its, the intimate circle people are prevent-its. These people play a crucial role in the success of the performer, and their qualifications are more daunting than the other three. You cannot pay your way into this circle. You have to *earn* your way into it. It is in this circle that major emotional deposits are more important than money deposits, even though both are welcome.

The intimate circle is comprised mostly of family members, and friends who are sometimes lifetime friends, that breathe the same intensity of drive, vision, and hunger as do their superstar friends. They are keepers of the flame, as well as preservers of the talent. When the world looks like a massive jungle to the performer, the intimate circle are the ones to clear the brush out, and offset the noise and confusion by providing civility, balance, and clarity to that person.

While their role is not that of an associates circle, per se, good management skills are required and needed for them to be helpful to the performer. Whether it is in the form of the skills obtained by the associates group or others that complement the performer's style in organizing schedules, time management, or adopting rest and pause sequences as an essential part of their duty in preserving the performer's integrity, all is meant to enhance their role as personal managers. And like all good managers—as good stewards of the craft—this requires management discipline.

A good example of management discipline is found in James E. Loehr's training and preparation of Olympic Gold medalist speed skating champion Dan Jensen. His book *Stress for Success,* is an excellent read for industrious managers who aspire to adopting schedules, routines, rituals, and plans in support of their clients. The quick reaction to unwanted distractions is a key criterion for a skill support system manager and one that requires patience.

Therefore it will take a discipline manager to identify those nuances that can wreck a performer's confidence and erode his skills if a trained consistent mentor does not temper him or her. Likewise, it becomes the intimate circle's job to catch those nuances when the performer might feel vulnerable, by holding a mirror to their face and correct those fallacies. However, there is also a caveat to the intimate circle influence: Since they are holding up a mirror to the performer's weakness and corrections, who is holding up the mirror to them? It might seem plausible that the support system embodies the same qualities or characteristics as the performer. As earlier discussed, intimate circle personnel may have the same skills as the associates circle; it is nothing unusual for a personal friend to be one's attorney, accountant, publicist, and/or business manager. These kinds of arrangements happen all the time. It is, therefore, important to separate the clarity of the position from the system of care skills offered by the intimate circle. At least the intimate circle person should have some emotional skills that the performer may be lacking, or contributing skills that enhance the performer. But as has been pointed out in this book, many such people are "entourages"—I use this term in a generic sense, because it alludes to persons who are friends, sometimes from childhood, who linger around their superstar performers because of some long-held favor that they feel is owed to them. These individuals, unfortunately, have held on far too long. What happens in these situations—and it has proven to be true, some of the time—is that the entourage of friends obtains more of the goodies than they are entitled to or deserve. In addition, what further happens is that what they receive tends to border on theft.

So therefore, having a well-matched intimate circle of friends is crucial to the strength, dignity, and integrity of the performer, and how or what they contribute to the organization becomes even more important.

Be a Solution-Giver

Every relationship is one of give and take. People may give their service in exchange for money or gifts, but the flow of that relationship must reflect individuals working in harmony in order to assure success for the performer.

Members of an organization have the responsibility to keep an eye on the performer's ball (his good fortune); that means protecting and harnessing a good conducive environment for that to happen. That does not mean stealing the ball, abusing it, or using it. In some organizations, this remains the case, and the reason might turn out to be a lack of maturity in running the performer's organization. Such immaturity becomes a perfect recipe for destroying the vision. Why do organizations fail to provide the right stuff? It might be because particular individuals within the circle haven't paid the price in working through their own deep issues. Friends, family, and close associates who lack principle-centered values can erode the client's vision. Even before an intimate circle member can become a contributor to the management team, he or she must match well with the performer's value system.

There is a number of ways in which a person contributes to the intimate circle. One simple way is to identify the strength of each player and position them in the organization accordingly. Today's organizations, whether small or large, are populated with individuals who should hold significant skills important to the superstar's career and life. If a friend or family member has strong math or organizational skills, they should be ready to accept additional training from continuing education. A brother who has great communication skills must and should employ all the tools available to improve this skill. Each person has been placed in his or her square, in a way that enhances the organization's chance of balance. A healthy and complete organization should be moving in a great deal of activity for their superstar friend or family member, where there is no time to stop. Therefore, no entourage should apply.

When one frames the above relationship, it is easy to infer where there may be a convergence of intimate friendships and invaluable skill workers contributing that makes sense. Here, there is a trade-off where dividends are deposited. Then again, handholding, being a keen listener and a wise and intuitive confidante are skills too. Accepting the distinction here versus the mere sideshows representing carefree playfulness—referring to those skills mentioned—requires maturity to accomplish, along with good character. In the long run, more than anything, character still remains the threshold. In addition, having patience and listening skills are important to the bedrock of the intimate circle to the superstar performer, more than any other part of the relationship.

Matrix #8: Community
"The Ties That Bind"

I waited to discuss community last because, in my mind, this matrix has bound together many superstar performers. Community happens to be a quality that is in the "eye of humanity." That is to say, performers often spend their affluent capital on areas that interest them and have personally touched their lives. What's more, they have submerged themselves in everyday problems of everyday people, where the lives of people come together. Part of the community involves an expansive model. In my opinion, there are two different views of community to be considered: one is often viewed narrowly, and the other one broadly. In the narrow sense, this includes responsibility to the people in the immediate proximity, including family, friends, and neighborhood. In the broader sense, it will include a commitment to a wider and larger commonality, virtually universal, appealing to many. This might include support of AIDS or cancer research, hunger or poverty initiatives, and/or building houses for the less fortunate, such as the work done by Habitat for Humanity. In all of these cases, one can see community at work.

The Oxford American Dictionary & Thesaurus defines community as "a group of people living together in one place, or a group of people with a common religion." Webster's dictionary defines it slightly differently, but in the same vein, as a "body of people, sharing in common good, and interest." This definition, however, might bring one closer to that module. But as I have mentioned before, there are two views of community to consider, and they aren't viewed equally. An individual can be seen broadly as all things to all people, becoming a pillar of the community, and still be deficient in the narrower community. He or she can be deficient as a father, as a loving spouse, or as a friend…or even deficient as a human being overall.

Yet most superstar performers on all levels have managed to balance both forms of community successfully, giving their already high-profile status an even greater boost. Nevertheless, for our purpose here, a broader context would be appropriate in making our general point about community. Instead of identifying community in divided pockets, the best way to view it, I feel, is through a universal prism. Viewing it in that context gave me a simpler way to examine it. This was not in any way taking away from their narrower contribution—including family, friends, and acquaintances—but their broader contributions were seen as well-documented.

For instance, many well known performers and athletes, and others used their celebrity to fight the ills of prejudice and segregation during the 1950s and 1960s. One actress used her fame for years in her charitable contributions to famine relief. With intense passion, she represented the organization, her dedication perhaps stemming from experiences she endured as a child. Another became a major advocate for AIDS research. Others have established philanthropic foundations in support of educational endeavors.

Several rock and roll stars have become best-known as philanthropic performers. Most have discovered that their talents can make a great difference in the lives of others. Many have participated in Band Aid, third-world debt relief, and raising awareness of the plight of Africans, including the AIDS pandemic.

Many agents of athletes have insisted as a condition of their representation that there be inserted in the contracts a clause binding their clients to a particular cause of their choice. Whether these performers channel their influence or their cash to a local endeavor or a universal one, it is meant to establish the "ties that bind."

In reading the memoir of one person that I have come across, I cannot help but think that his approach, attitudes, and life philosophy became shaped by the experiences he witnessed growing up in the segregated South. He frequently details, with great admiration, his close friendships with African-American families with whom he grew up, observing the obvious unfairness plaguing those families' lives. These Eureka moments, "sowed a seed" in his conscience. The so-called "separate but equal" facilities and the inadequate accommodations in education and housing gave him reason to believe that every American should be entitled to affordable housing. The ties that bind led him to be a supporter of building houses.

The effect that Habitat for Humanity had on individuals and families became a national and international one. His efforts have changed lives in an intimate way, by touching and feeling the lives of the individuals close up, but one can also conclude that he changed lives on a global scale as well. In theory, many famous superstar performers active community outreach that becomes national and/or global due to the mere persona of their fame. Whatever move is made by one of these performers will more than likely magnify tenfold.

One may be tempted to ask, in spite of the good deeds these performers contribute to their community, how does this relate to their greatness? One answer that comes to mind—though there are many—is that superstar performers' talents are seen as a means to an end. Their profession is not who they are, but what is important is how the profession has helped them expand their humanity. In other words, what they do as a profession does not define them. In fact, the opposite is true; the achievements reflect their love for humanity and ultimately "community."

Of course, some might quibble that all well-known people who are involved in community would necessarily be great because of it, and this may be true. The common error is that they do not always stay great in the minds of many without it, either. It boils down to one simple fact and it remains that what bridges our humanity is common to us all, and binds us all together. Need I say more?

Section III

How to Build a Superstar Performer from the Ground Up

"And the city lieth foursquare and the length is as large as the breadth: and he measured the city with the reed, twelve thousand furlongs. The length and the breadth and the height of it are equal."

~Revelation 21:16

December 23, 2011: 8:30 p.m.

I sit here at home in my study and I am finishing the remaining touches on my New Year's goals. This ritual supports a long-standing practice that has served me well on many fronts, and I am sure it has also served others. I have gained a great sense of self-satisfaction and reward from these exercises, in the way that I can look back after an entire year and see what progress has developed. In addition, it became a fun thing to do when extracting, adding, and amending items, some after close introspection, which I no longer found necessary to my general vision for my life. And of course this is okay, because through the various schedules, charts, errands, re-evaluations and amendments to my plans, I am kept focused on where I am, where I should be, and whether what I am doing matches the real intent of my heart and mind. The weeding-out of defective analysis was necessary in order to construct what I thought to be that perfect plan. But is there really a perfect plan? I still kept in the back of my mind, however, that things rarely work out according to plan. I knew well enough that life is not this way, where one fits things into small compartments and they turn out the way you expect. I also believe that the best-laid plans are better than no plans at all, and are necessary in building foundational excellence. It relates to the excellence that cues one in to everyday habits that make a superstar performer perform with ease.

Foundational excellence is found when healthy habits are practiced on a daily basis to support the inherent mission of the person. These habits are skill training practices, but they are also "life spring" practices, which may include early-morning meditation, physical fitness routines, emotional stimulation or renewal exercises, or other sustaining measures. These qualities are building blocks at the core of building a superstar performer—or, for that matter, a human being conditioned to live a quality life with a foundation for efficient and productive work.

What Does Success Look Like to You?

The other day I read an article entitled "How to live to 100, starting today." I was intrigued by the article for many reasons. I had read numerous articles over the years that gave similar declarations as sworn testimonies of true secrets to long life. The difference was that this article referenced as its source those who have lived their lives fully, those who were now 100. I thought there is no better testimonial than this. What the article addressed were certain commonsense approaches to a wholesome quality of life: Drink enough water each day, think good thoughts, walk regularly, breathe deeply, and have good and healthy friendships: all necessities to balanced living.

Yet, several years prior to the discovery of this article, I witnessed my own personal experience with a potential centenarian; I posed the same question to him. Except here, for the most part, it started in a different way. It began with the question, "What is the secret to a long, healthy, and successful life?" Mr. Frederickson, I will call him, is someone whom I have known since my childhood. In fact, he was ordained a deacon in the church my father pastored for nearly twenty years. I have fond memories of him as that of a tall lean man who dressed well, with a special habit, when in church, of sitting with his legs crossed, and folding his arms underneath the one leg. I thought, at the time, that this was the most dignified image I had ever seen. Of course, as I grew older, the image of this elegant and slender tall figure became foggier, so that even the few pounds he had gained over the years might have gone undetected by me.

On this particular occasion, I now saw him as an older man—much grayer, of course—coming down the church steps one Sunday, when I asked him what must be one of life's most mysterious questions.

"What is the secret to a long, healthy, and successful life?" Caught off guard by my question, he chuckled. Then, regaining his composure, he responded.

"Hard work. Hard work never hurt anyone.

"Eat well. You must fuel your body with healthy and good things.

"Sleep well. Getting the proper sleep ensures readiness for the next day.

"Don't worry over the small stuff."

After listening to him, I mused, "Is that all there is to it?" Of course, I knew better. Genetics perhaps played a small role, as did an active spiritual life. What's more, his attitude made the difference. Mr. Frederickson, nevertheless, passed at 99 but his wife—Mrs. Frederickson—is still living, and as of this writing, has reached the spirited age of 102. A lifelong loving partnership is another of their secrets as well. Peace of mind, I would think, is another. For the most part, I consider the Frederickson's to be superstar performers, so that these pages should include their contributions.

Again, let us consider the analysis related to the term of superstardom. The range of adjectives is enormous in defining the term, and the words usually qualitative in terms of size. How big this person is compared to that person. How famous is this one compared the other, or how enormously wealthy this person is compared to this one in comparison to this to that…and it goes on and on. These limited phrases are marginalizing in terms of fame, money, prestige, clothing, houses, boats, cars, land, resources, how good-looking is your daughter compared to my daughter, etc. This range of superficial offerings fails to properly define superstardom in its highest form, but instead, references the act as "keeping up with the Joneses."

For though it is safe to say that some superstar performers are relatively well-off, it is equally true that they relied less on their wealth in defining themselves. With the exception of many others whose lives were dedicated to meager endeavors, but were able to wield successfully humility and power in the same breath, many others, as I can attest, made good livings. There are several people who are definitely super rich…as super rich as they come, and well-respected in the business world who would ever dispute their superstardom in other ways. Many live frugal, but have the means to build gazillion-dollar homes, but chose not to and live normal and consistent lives. Some are completely deserving of a claim to superstardom—not to mention their integrity is unquestionably above reproach in the world of business.

The Frederickson's, however, were married for nearly eighty years, worked hard, were involved in the community, were spiritually viable to themselves, their family, and the community, yet lacked the wealth or influence that the others in this book have aspired to or enjoyed. However, they were superstars. Many were spiritually devout people who took their spiritual life seriously, praying and reading scriptures daily and living simple lives, but remained captains in their on vocations, inspiring countless numbers of men and women today who are superstars themselves.

Yet, we would be wrong in believing that achievement alone is the criterion by which to measure superstardom, without including other important qualities. We have come to measure success in volumes because we have conditioned ourselves to see it in that way, instead of perceiving it in the tiniest of situations around us.

On one hand, we are conditioned to view a famous football player, actor, or actress in terms of superstardom, but when we find that their private realities run counter to their public ones, we are less inclined to question it. On the other hand, a teacher who has taught for several decades, and who is shown to have the classic qualities and traits outlined in this book, will find less respect for their talents than those who appear on television and make fools of themselves. For some inexplicable reason, these individuals seem to wield more power in influencing others than they should. Why is this?

While we are on the subject of teachers, I believe they represent the true superstars. My mother is a retired teacher. To many of us, this theory is undeniable. The concept of teacher as hero brings up a debate, especially since our country, in its current state, is facing an economic crisis, and the solution for some facets of that crisis is to seek job training and additional education.

The central premise of the debate now is teachers' pay. Good conscience convinces us, and in some manner morally, that we should defend a teachers' pay hike. I agree, by reasonable accounts, that teachers' compensation is inadequate. We will at least agree on that point. But instead of advocating this view, we undermine our support of it by *compartmentalizing it in our psyche that it does matter—but in a way, it does not.* We twist a web of contradictions that is inevitably inconsistent with our own values. The result of this inconsistency is a lack of moral courage to act; we do not petition the powers that be to change the situation. Instead, we cherry-pick what or who deserves superstardom.

Throughout this book, the intention was to distinguish between those who labor at their chosen art and those who choose to labor on the cheap, to scheme and swindle success their way. By far, it is the single most important theme in understanding true superstardom. With that in mind, I came away knowing what to put my time into. But it took a series of errors in my own life to reach this point, to put priorities where they should be, evaluate my intentions, closely scrutinize partnerships in business, friendships, girlfriends, and even a wife, while deepening my resolve regarding what I should look for. What qualities would I find suitable/desirable, and which would meet my deepest value-driven principles? It became simple as that—but less simple than that. What it required of me, instead, was a level of maturity which, at the time, I emotionally and spiritually lacked, but also defined for me what I expected of those who led me and those whom I led.

Adopted as a personal management manual, working on this book reaffirmed other truths that I had always known, but did not fully practice. I discovered that everyday conditioning, which most performers find necessary in *bringing life to their vision,* cements their core. This core often includes physical, emotional, mental, and spiritual exercises that provide not only a secure, solid foundation to work from, but also a gateway to true freedom. It simply requires practice. In other words, to be equipped for the battle at hand, you must build your life where you are, inside-out, block by block from ground up every day in ways that give discipline, direction, and meaning to your life. This kind of pattern remains the quintessential hallmark of effective performers. Thus, in the remaining pages, I am going to outline a plan that is consistent with the spirit of many superstar performers, as well as of many others.

Let Freedom Ring

"The price of freedom is eternal vigilance."—Thomas Jefferson

One of the guys I know who works at my gym is a competitive bodybuilder. He is not yet at a professional level, but he desires one day to reach that goal. We work out daily, sometimes twice a day. Other times we work on different plans. Granted, this routine appears to be a bit over the top, yet keep in mind that its function is to reach certain physical goals, and to create evolving conditions. On this particular day, he and I observed a limited number of patrons at the gym and cited—prior to that day—a decreased number of attendees.

"It's sure thin in here," I said. John turned to me and smiled. In fact, we both smiled.

"This happens every year around this time. As we get closer to the holidays, some of those people slack off and vow to return at the beginning of the year, trying to get into shape for the spring and summer."

When one thinks conceptually of core foundations, one is referring to concepts requiring a super level of commitment and discipline, which those who commit "some time" cannot gasp. This lack of commitment, and the person's failed attempts, may be due to motives and intentions being driven by superficial impulsiveness. Impulsiveness is driven by the lesser self, or their cues are not strong enough to make the necessary change.

Let us say there are individuals who desire to get into shape with the sole intent to fit into a wedding dress or a swimsuit. This could be seen as an encouraging and noble pursuit, and it might lead to an epiphany for one to take better care of oneself, as well, because the benefits gives them energy to spring *life into their vision*. However, if the experience stops at the watershed, then their intentions will remain at a rudimentary level and more than likely will not be appropriate for an effective performer.

While we may all, from time to time, neglect certain routine healthy habits that give life to our vision, there are only a few who can accomplish working out every day, as do a few famous fitness icons. Those who have a manifest interest in becoming an effective performer do so through steady and consistent maintenance of the core foundational areas of their lives, where they were able to build their vision. Those core foundations are how one strengthens one's spiritual, physical, emotional, and mental life. It is only through training these areas correctly that one can experience true freedom.

Rituals of Superstar Performers

Approximately 70% of self-help books written today have indicated that a path toward greatness begins with some basic rituals adopted by superstar performers in order to give them a better chance for success.

Some actors read their scripts in complete silence in privacy without anyone interrupting him. They rehearsed the script in a manner effective for the role.

One well known person I know instructed her staff with various routines and schedules meant to keep them strong. She prescribed to a repeated pattern, and habits formed in order to condition their lives. One other person got up early, as well, and exercised, ate the same low-fat diet, and maintained this routine for seven decades.

Many highly successful coaches I know follow a script with their players by executing practice drills designed to allow them to become the best-conditioned players on the court when they faced their opponents. These coaches follow a ritual of preparation, meditation, condition, which no doubt was incorporated into their game plan of success.

One novelist, I am told, wakes up at 4:00 every morning and works for five to six hours. In the afternoon, he either runs a 10km or swims for 1500k. He reads some, listens to music, and goes to bed at 9:00. These kinds of rituals served him well during the six-month period during which he wrote his new novel. He has said that the experience "mesmerizes him to reach a deeper state of mind." Coincidentally, there is an unusual correlation between the conditioning process prescribed above and that advocated by addiction specialists. As a juvenile justice administrator, I know too well the long-term effort required for clients to break a bad habit and learn a healthy one. In working with many specialists and consulting with them on the mechanics of addiction disease treatment, the general view highlights the importance of long-term treatment. They believe—as I do—that it takes from eighteen months to two years for an addict to make significant changes in their behavior, belief system, frame of reference, humility, and brain chemistry in order for them to rinse the stench of the disease from their being. Anything shorter than that after an initial detoxification, and the chance for relapse becomes a greater possibility. Furthermore, if that addicted person shows few signs of change in his environment as to adopting new and healthy support systems—something I have extensively shared in the book—the chances are likely that recovery will fail.

Similar reasoning is found when a support staff, in and around a superstar's life, lack the healthy core-foundational skills necessary to provide cohesiveness. Constructing an environment for growth where everyone is aware of the same plan, and same line of vision, requires team effort. Whether it is Team Alicia, Team Steve, Team Gloria, or Team Jennifer, if any part of the team is not on the same page that you may be on, elimination of some members will be required in order to find balance within the organization. Therefore, it is widely advised that the team members be as disciplined in the core-foundation areas as the superstar performer is.

Furthermore, one must not forget that strengthening core-foundational skills is as essential as strengthening the performer's talent skills. For instance, one writer has made comparisons of his writing rituals to similar preparation related to the physical, mental, and spiritual discipline required to run a marathon.

If you took the five to six hours of writing that the novelist did and multiply it per day, week, or six months, one would probably attain almost close to the 10,000 hours of mastery that is defined in the book *Outliers*. Moreover, reaching this level of proficiency lends itself to only a small number of people achieving it, because it takes enormous work and stamina. Yet far too often, the road to true mastery becomes the road less traveled, and many choose the road to easy gains. A number of people choose this road because it delivers quick stardom without deserving it. We have seen this many times with people who are chosen to be on a popular reality show. When they are chosen, most are unprepared for the attention that will come their way. When they begin to receive attention from the producers, the viewing audience and agents who seek to represent them, they become overwhelmed by it that they turn into narcissistic monsters.

Naturally, the lavishing of sudden attention upon a person gives them confidence that they are special, when deep down, they know it is not deserved or earned.

Rule #1: "Keep Your Mind in Perfect Peace"

Adopted from the famous Biblical scripture of the prophet Isaiah that states "You will keep in perfect peace him whose mind is steadfast, because he trusts in you," simply put, the activities that you do each day will bring you closer to keeping your mind and body strong and agile for the fight. This is a building block and it includes a terrain of events that many people have used to strengthen their lives. I personally start my day with a combination of rituals that I believed have strengthened my spirit, mind, and body.

I wake up at around 5:00, drink a cold glass of water, and begin to meditate for between 15-20 minutes. This meditation session may include simple silence, scripture, yoga, or inspirational passages from a book—anything that I feel warms my mind and spirit. I will next take any necessary vitamins or supplements, and I am off to the gym for an hour. I will return home, take a shower, and eat a hearty nutritional breakfast. Even before I walk into my office, I have already accomplished several things sustaining in my life that reflect my spiritual, mental, and physical self. Therefore, throughout the day I feel tempered and fueled by a natural ebb and flow.

Others can invest in light-hearted activities like watching old black and white movies that give them a feeling of euphoria, or the comedic relief of a good comedy. Many have found leisure time in watching college football games, as I do, on Saturday's. These exciting events on many weekends in the fall allow friends and like-spirited individuals to fellowship together and enjoy each others company. The laughter, the competitive drive amongst a group of friends, and the festive enjoyment of eating great food and having fun is made by the fact that life's special moments bring emotional and mental relief. The factors to consider here require developing activities warranted to strengthening, ones emotional, mental, spiritual and moral core. One such person who developed a recovery plan when he was diagnosed with a serious illness consisted of mega doses of Vitamin C, along with equal doses of a positive attitude, and an environment of healthy people surrounding him. He took deliberate action to laugh aloud, to help relieve the tensions that might expedite further illnesses.

He dedicated himself to a complete spectrum of healthy activities, all meant to safeguard his heart and mind from any stresses that deterred his progress. Forming a mosaic cocktail of activities aimed to nurturing one's mind, heart, and soul is always a right-headed direction. Even if you must run a gazillion miles, read an inspiring poem that lightens your soul, listen to inspiring music, pray until you cannot pray any more, shout, and/or scream, do what is required to take your spirit to the place you deserve. Do it as consistently as it can be done.

Rule #2: Demand and Expect That Your Support System Be Healthy in Core-Foundational Skills

Support groups must be healthy in the core foundations too. We know this to be true in everyday living. Furthermore, it would be great if these support group representatives were all family members, but this is not always the case because they may not all be a healthy system. In fact, other support systems can show up at any number of times in a superstar's life. They can be friends, who grew up together, or business partnerships formed later, who share similar values, habits, work ethics, drive, and vision. On the other hand, they can be mentors who give good counsel and advice on a variety of different fronts. In any event, what the superstar performer might be requesting is seen as a tall order, since everyone tends to grow and mature differently, at different rates, and on different emotional timetables. Overall, though, there must be some growth occurring. Even small growth can make a difference, if it is in the right direction. Part of enhancing that growth can occur by making opportunities for growth available to the support system.

The impact the support system has on you can mean the difference between life and death to your career, your mind, and in some cases your life. Yet, by having only yes-men in your corner can be emblematic of the problem and damaging to the ultimate goal.

Similarly, it is equally important that the superstar support the supporters. Educating them in areas that will enhance both themselves and the superstar will make the supporter more responsible, more accepting of their task and future, and less likely to jeopardize the security they've been afforded. They will be more focused on preserving what they have, and deepening their commitment to the organization.

Rule #3: Work Diligently on Your God-given Talent

Some people have the innate ability to connect to people with their special concern for others. These people recognized this as their primary gift, but were also acutely aware of other abilities to manage people, and work daily on merging these two abilities. Their managerial skills were proven over time in balance of one's emotion with the needs of the people who they serve which is, in my opinion, comparable to any well-run organization.

These people are able to exercise their talent for motivating people, by helping them to see the big picture of their contributions. In truth, their greatest gift becomes a moral one. Their aim is to teach those around them not only to exercise long-suffering, but condition them to endure what they encountered in their walk.

I am aware of individuals in my own life who epitome strong work ethics, who by creating foundations and executing fundamentals to achieve success, have the capacity to cue in on subtle opportunities, which employed seizing moments in the blink of an eye and knowing when to act and not to.

Whatever your special skill might be, use it to your advantage. What you lack in innate ability, supplement with the practical gains that God has given us all. Thus, the capacity of our gifts determines where our focus will be and where we can align our contributions. You love what you love because you love it, but our dreams can be made easier if we focus on what works best for us.

Rule #4: Have a Solid Support System—They Are Your Guardian Angels

The explanations made relating to support systems, thus far, have been in preserving the superstar's talent, but there is a greater aim for which preserving the superstar is more important. While most of the time the support system spends a majority of their time enhancing the talent of the superstar performer, a portion of their time is spent protecting them from the wolves and the "imps" of the world. You may ask, what are "imps"? I was taken aback by this word one day when my Aunt Rayanne spoke of it. It refers to individuals whose main purpose is to steal your good work. Imps are categorized in the Bible as evil spirits (Satan's angels). The intimate circle of friends' duty is to protect the superstars from these individuals who are the gatekeepers to the heart, the mind, and the soul of the superstar.

Stardom of any kind, ordinarily, will attract most people, including those with undesirable goals and those who are starved for attention. Moreover, the attractive gifts of those who come with undesirable goals are actually unattractive because they end up corrupting the circle and eroding what has been built for years. The rule here is always simply: Know your friends and identify the ones that will do you harm.

Furthermore, it is worth reminding you at this point again, that talent alone does not make a superstar. There are enormously talented people who are now working at meat-packing factories, and not necessarily in managerial positions, but as laborers. A few stock shelves in Wal-Mart, and those same ones might have as much ability to run a division of that corporation as the ones who are currently running it. Nevertheless, what distinguishes these individuals from others may just come down to a lack of drive, opportunity, and support mechanisms to take their talent further. Though the need to succeed requires a support system, having the right support system means more.

Rule # 5: Take Responsibility for Your Life and Your Actions

Superstar performers take responsibility for their actions and lives. Most superstar performers do not pity themselves for the unfortunate thing that happens to them. They fight, take charge of their lives, circumstances, shortcomings, or struggles, and remained determined that they—not others—held their destiny.

Those superstar performers never wasted time with futile posturing, or succumbed to defensive attitudes that derailed their vision. Nor was there resentment, licking of wounds, holding grudges, or a blaze of contempt. They all stayed in their lane, intent on being so laser-focused on the prize that if they were to walk into the noisiest factory, they would not be the least distracted. Rather, their concentration remained strong as steel, with the determination to forge ahead.

It is a testament to the human spirit when we hear of stories told of persons arriving in this country from another with knowing very few English words and succeeding against unmistakable odds. These individuals take on odd jobs as washing dishes and sweeping floors to support themselves, to find themselves in the evenings being tutored in the English language. It is even more impressive when some of these individuals use of their special talent succeeds beyond expectations, and their abilities help to improve the lives of millions of people. These actions in any ones book are not just great, they are noble.

Some others took similar approaches in taking charge of their own personal health by committing to change their eating habits and creating exercise regimens that worked best for them. They also adhered to much the same standard of personal responsibility advocated by those in motivating individuals to reclaim their lives. In all these instances, personal ownership and responsibility became the one key to their success.

Rule #6: Have a Plan for Every Day of Your Life

When speaking of the phrase, "Plan every day of your life," it actually means aligning oneself around a set of spiritual, physical, emotional, and mental principles in living out your best self. By most accounts, this planning is commonplace amongst superstar performers, both those I have mentioned in this book, and others.

Planning, however, in this case, is not just fly-by-night planning. Instead, it requires a certain amount of concentration that is as steady as yoga moves and requires relentless patience to execute. It is the kind one often thinks of when envisioning Alexander Bell ensconced in the basement of his house, working practically those 10,000 hours to perfect his art and enjoy the rewards of his efforts. Except the story does not end there, because for every Alexander Bell who personifies the planning, drive, ambition, and vision that propels such people to greatness, there is another who will chase cheap achievement, and figure it can be accomplished with inertia.

Unfortunately, of course, we know from the law of physics, inertia is resistance to motion, action, or change—and some people also have this resistance. I know this fact too well, since my present position involves counseling and advising young people and their families in ways to better their lives. Gang members are considered resistant to adopting plans that might alter their lives for the better, but find it more rewarding to play shoot-em-up because it lacks thinking or imagination. In other words, it takes less thought to point and then shoot. Young people who drop out of school cannot seem to grasp that the planning and discipline required to stay in school will be no different from the planning and discipline required for any of the alternatives. The fact remains that the planning of superstars on an everyday basis is never an unusual happening for them; it is necessary, a prerequisite for how and why they do what they do. Of course, it's not that they plan every minute of their lives, but it does come close. What most super-performers subscribe to is a plan that is structural in nature, by which their goals, routines, and schedules can receive the most velocity in the shortest period. The structure is similar to the Triangle Offense of the Los Angeles Lakers, in which the players were able to utilize their best skills and talents within a system. It becomes a system where schedules, routines, and rituals work within a framework, enough so that they enhance, not starve, one's progress. For Instance, many highly driven individuals adopt similar structure of habit forming as others. They all relied on substantive practices that enhanced their innate abilities—and so can you, by tuning in to those foundational areas needing the most work. As a footnote, there are plenty of materials out there that can serve in giving you direction in your own personal quest. Here, I have only scraped the surface.

Rule # 7: Nurture the Community in You

Community is one of the basic tenets of superstars. In my opinion, it is the spring from which all things flow. I believe that the meaning of our lives comes into better focus when we are able to share it with others. Our connection to the world finds satisfaction in ways that goal-driven striving and grasping fail to do. Without community, we will soon die off the vine or be forced to ask the questions: "What is this all for? Is it really all about me?"

Many of us have been confronted with the same question and have had to ask the question "What is it all about?" Is it all about you? The many superstar performers, whom I have researched, felt less so. Instead, they were able to reconcile that selfish side of themselves through self-help, but were later inclined to see their lives in a much broader prism that brought wholeness to their being, enabling them to feel and touch lives in unexpected ways.

What draws us to each other, after all, is our humanity—that special quality that meets at the axis of living a life with cause and purpose, and then in the end, refreshes, replenishes, and feeds our souls. Community is meant to make us feel that way. Yet, little is written on how one should achieve that community. There is no formula for achieving that community as long as it's authentic and heartfelt.

I have demonstrated community myself in working and helping young people and their families, performing acts of community-building in my place of faith and in the confines of the intimate circles around me. I confess I could do more, but I also live with it as much as others who are committed to their community. Yet, I believe this community goes beyond than what one does at home or in their local community in general. It is much easier for us to accept the idea that doing half-baked activities that lack conviction qualify as true community. In my opinion, these half measures qualify only as paper tigers. But the community that I am referring to helps us understand a particular plight of a person, become empathetic to it or its situation, when the more we can appreciate its significances in our own lives, we can then better draw a broader understanding from it by placing ourselves in their shoes.

The community that advances the moral cause of our superstars is indeed value-driven. The early quest of their decisions that attract them to certain community activities is found embedded in a philosophy that encompasses the depth and breadth of their being. Does a man's Christian faith influence his missionary zeal to advocate for the rights of others by employing the teaching of civil disobedience and non-violence? A number of women talk show hosts would have been unprepared to become a champion for women had their experiences not dictated it, nor would an advocate for women amplifying voice for women be heard had she not experience some degrade of women in her past. These individuals, and many more, were spot-on regarding what their community looked liked to them, and they embodied it in everything that they did.

Parting Words...

As you have discovered, I have focused on only a few examples of well-known and famous people, but this was only a way to make a specific point. Granted, I have mentioned a number of others who weren't. But we all have to admit that most people relate to well-known people much more easily, because they want to know how they are able to achieve their status in life and, consequently, how someone else might emulate their success. Furthermore, you will have noticed that throughout this book, superstardom has rarely been synonymous with riches, fame, and power. Instead, I was able to keep my focus on genuine and authentic attributes of superstardom, with the attention less weighted on material aspects.

I found that although one should cherish the superstar performer's achievements, one should also cherish the superstar's mentors. We should cherish, as well, their 5th-grade English teacher, or the high school or college drama instructor who encouraged their talent. We should cherish the math teacher who lit our minds about math that, at first glance, frightened us. We should cherish the Sunday school teacher whose life exemplified integrity in not only words, but also deeds; or the coach who pushed you to the limit and got out of you more than you realized was in you—and above all, the people who helped nurture your soul. This is what superstardom really looks like.

My bet would be that if you looked around their neighborhood, or down your street, you would find your superstar. Whether influenced by those who are famous or humble, rich or poor, distinguished or undistinguished, privileged or unprivileged, there is in some way, somehow, and somewhere that a superstar nudged them along. My hope, however, is that many will come along, as others have and become *in a world of their own*. So with this said, I bid you adieu...

Sources and References

Chapter 3: Skill Trainers v. Non-Skill Trainer

1. *Creating Minds,* by Howard Gardner, Basic Books 1994. Book and reference is given to briefly emphasis skill training.
2. *On The Waterfront,* Columbia Pictures, 1954. Movie cited, but no detail given of scene. The work used in furthering examines a point in the text.

Chapter 6: Matrix 4, Preparation

1. Plato's recitation, "The first and best victory is for a man to conquer himself". Quotation has long been in the public domain.

Chapter 8: Matrix 6, Talent

1. *Talent is Overrated,* by Geoff Colvin, Penguin Group, 2010. Work cited as a reference. No permission is required.

Chapter 9: Matrix 7, Support System

1. *Stress for Success,* by James Loehr, Crown Publishing Group, 1997. Work is mention as a related read and reference.

Chapter 10: Matrix 8, Community.

1. *The Oxford American Dictionary and Thesaurus.* Citing the definition of the term, "Community"

Chapter 18, "How to Build a Superstar Performer from the Ground-up"

1. *Outlier,* by Malcolm Gladwell, Little Brown & Company, 2008. Cited and mentioned.

CPSIA information can be obtained at www.ICGtesting.com
Printed in the USA
LVOW06s0510051113

359977LV00001B/82/P